FIRST, KNOW WH

WHAT YOU WANT

FIRST, KNOW WHAT YOU WANT

Why Goals Don't Work and How To Make Them

ANDREW HALFACRE

FIRST, KNOW WHAT YOU WANT

First published in Great Britain 2011
by Bookshaker.com

ISBN 978-1-9074985-5-8

For the rest of us.

Table of Contents

Foreword

Much of my career over the last two decades has been based on processes that I learned through NeuroLinguistic Programming (NLP). In consultancy, facilitation and coaching I find these really powerful, and a select few are regular members of my toolkit.

But it nearly did not happen. There is a process called "Setting well formed outcomes". This is so powerful that when I first give out the sheet of eight questions I tell people that this could be the most valuable sheet of paper they will ever touch.

The first question requires people to say what they want. It has to be stated in the positive.

You would think that was simple enough. But when I did my NLP Certificate test nearly 20 years ago, I failed on this very question. The key is to recognise what you want – and not what you don't want. Repeatedly I answered what I didn't want, I couldn't understand the difference and I failed the test. Unless I passed this test I could not have gone on to the further training that has formed the basis for my business.

Fortunately, two of the trainers took me aside and after several attempts I suddenly saw the light, and they gave me my certificate.

Focusing on what you *do* want is key to coaching. Before you can *have* what you want, you must *know* what you want.

Unfortunately, finding out is often not as simple as it seems and knowing what you want in life can be a major challenge.

The core purpose of Brefi Group is to "help individuals and teams in organisations discover and achieve their potential so that they can be more effective with less stress". It is our passion to help people achieve their potential, but first they must discover it.

Coaches and other professionals in the personal development field may well make it their life's work to decide their mission and purpose. However, this is much less likely to be true for their clients.

Andrew Halfacre has been our lead trainer for many years and has noticed how few of his coaching clients and people attending his courses have spent much time addressing this apparently simple question – "What do you really want?"

In fact, many have never considered it at all. But, before we can help someone achieve a goal, we need tools to help them understand and know what they want.

Andrew set out to identify and collect tools for this purpose.

First, Know What You Want is an important resource, not just for coaches, mentors and counsellors, but also for anyone who would love to really resolve their own mind what they want in life, work, and play.

Different approaches work best for different people and this book contains a range of different processes that will help you find out what you want.

And once you know, then (and only then) you will be able to set out to get it.

Richard Winfield
Founder and principal consultant
Brefi Group Limited
www.threeticks.com

Acknowledgements

Thank you for choosing this book. You belong to a very special group of people – those who are not willing to settle for what they have now. It's no coincidence that you have picked up this book because nearly 95% of the people I speak to would love to make up their mind about what they really want.

They can all tell me what they *don't* want but working out what they *do* want is much harder. If this is your experience, then thank you for joining me. It's a privilege to work together with you as you discover what you want and find the motivation to go after it.

There are many great coaches, consultants and trainers who have dedicated their lives to helping people do more, get more and be more. Eagle-eyed readers will spot themes and flavours of their work woven into the fabric of this book. In particular I'd like to thank Seth Godin, David Allen, Merlin Mann, Michael Neill and especially Steven Pressfield. Do take advantage of their books and resources which you'll find in the Resources section. To these giants who made it easier for me to see, thank you.

I'd also like to thank those whose practical help gave birth to this book: Joe, Lucy and Sylvia at Bookshaker and my ideal readers, Amanda Worsley, Allan Gifford and Richard Winfield. You made it a better book.

And the ultimate thanks of course to God, our maker, who breathed into us the breath of life so that alone among the animals we can reason and decide what we want. What a gift.

Permissions

Grateful thanks to Michael Neill for permission to quote from his regular coaching tips (www.supercoach.com) in the section on Mood and Desire.

Introduction

I was standing in front of the flipchart extolling the virtues of goal setting to a room full of young managers. As I explained the various techniques and started selling the benefits of clear, written, goals I could see eyes slowly dropping and faces closing. As I droned on and on, even I began to realise this wasn't quite the reaction I'd hoped for. So I stopped mid-sentence:

"What's wrong?"

After lots of foot shuffling and several attempts to avoid eye contact, one of them raised a hand.

"This is great, Andrew, but the problem is we don't know what we want. How can we set goals for the future if we don't know what we really want?"

I stopped right there. It had simply never occurred to me that they might not know. That night I put together a presentation for them: 'Four Ways To Know What You Want'. And the more I worked with clients, the more it became obvious that there is an epidemic of not knowing what we want. As demand for my presentation grew, it became the book you are holding.

If you are having trouble knowing what you want, then this is the book for you. In it you will find an insider's guide to knowing your own mind. You'll get direct practical help (that you cannot find elsewhere) and, if you wish, you will recover the motivation to go after it.

Who Should Read This Book?

If any of these statements sound familiar, this is for you:

- You know what you ***don't*** want but struggle to be clear about what you ***do*** want.

- You could do almost anything but you end up doing almost nothing because you lack the certainty to pick something.

- You don't like where you are but can't figure out where you should be.

- You know you are holding yourself back but you are not sure from what.

- You have let others make the bigger decisions about your life; you suspect you might be coasting.

- You carry around a vague but pressing feeling that there is something else for you, if only you could know what it is.

- When asked what you want, your mind goes blank or your heart starts racing. It scares you.

- You're facing a big decision and you don't know what to do, or you have a feeling you might know but are afraid of the answer.

- You're scared of making the changes that you know you could be making.

- Somehow, you know that your life would be different if only you could work out what you wanted.

Using It With Others

Maybe you are a parent or concerned friend looking to help someone decide what they want. Or a professional with clients who struggle to create a direction for themselves. You'll benefit from a wealth of insider tips and learn conversational stealth tools to help them help themselves. You'll be able to create change in others just by talking.

If You Don't Know What You Want, You Will Follow Someone Who Does

The facts are:

- Those who know what they want experience more clarity, better focus and higher levels of energy and success.

- If you don't know what you want then you will end up working for or following someone who does.

- Any time you are not hard at work on your agenda, you're working on somebody else's.

A Book For The Rest Of Us

Some people are born knowing what they want. As they grow they quickly embrace the idea of setting challenging goals and something ignites them to pursue those goals. Some grow to become sports stars, some politicians, some become over-excited motivational speakers and others end up as high-achieving business people. Almost all of them, if they gain financial success, publish a book laying out their philosophy of understanding what you want and pursuing it with determination. It all seems so easy.

Then there are the rest of us.

Our goals, if we think of them as such, are modest. A life partner, a family, making a small contribution, security. When challenged to say what we want, our most honest answer is that we don't know and if we do know then it's because we stumbled across it while doing something else. We can only stand aside slightly shamefaced as the motivated and driven yell about the process of goal setting. We tried it once and it didn't work.

This is a book for the rest of us...

Before You Can Have What You Want, You Need To Know What You Want

Before you can *have* what you want, you have to *know* what you want. That's what makes this book different from all the other self-help books out there.

This is not a book about the glory of setting goals. Neither is it a cheerleading book written to drive you to the heights of success. It's not a book about *getting*. It's a book about *being*. Being a person who knows who they are. Who knows themselves well enough to be clear about what they want and motivated enough to move towards it.

I'm simply going to help you work out, perhaps for the first time, what you want.

This is the book you should read *before* you read anything about how to 'sell more', 'score big' or 'move to the next level'.

Setting Goals Does Not Work For Most People

If you are wandering through life with a nagging sense that you could be doing more or you've actively tried to set goals for yourself without much success, this is the book for you. This is the book that will give you the missing piece that comes before goal setting.

There are myriad goal-setting books on the market and an equal number of goal-setting systems, each with its own fans.

Much of this ignores the plain truth that most people, when you ask them, don't know what they want. Goals, beyond a daily to-do list, are a hazy concept for most. An even greater mass of people have not made it as far as using an effective to-do list.

Why are these masses of people quite happy to let life pull them along, simply reacting to what turns up? Is it fear? Lack of a good technique?

Or simply that no one ever gave them permission to know what they want?

They follow the fashions of the day, driven by advertisers, politicians and the values of their friends while steadfastly ignoring their feeling that there has to be more.

I wrote this book to remedy this situation. If you've picked this up in a bookshop wondering whether it is for you then it probably is. It will help you know your own mind and then you can make a decision about which goal setting system you use to help you.

How Celebrities and Stars Make It Hard For Us

If I hear another famous person say, *"I knew when I was six years old that I wanted to be on the stage,"* I will scream. Why? Because they make it sound so easy, so effortless. They were six years old and, as they tell it, ambition floated down to rest on their shoulder, igniting a lifelong drive to get to where they are now.

We love these stories. We love them because they are so rare. To read about a celebrity *who always knew* comforts us. We can let ourselves off the hook because we don't know, we're not clear and ambition hasn't floated down on to our shoulders (or not so we've noticed). And yet. And yet...

Come And Sit By The Fire

There's something nagging at you isn't there? A vague feeling of discontent. A low internal murmur that you can hear at odd moments. A confession when alcohol loosens your tongue. You want something. Something other than what you've got. The trouble is that you do not know what it is but you have a suspicion. You suspect that if you could work it out then it would light a fire under your life.

And here you hover, half afraid of the fire, half drawn to its warmth. What will you do? Why not come in and sit down beside this fire for a while and let's see if we can help you figure it all out.

In the following pages I've distilled everything I know into a simple programme that will lead you step by step to knowing what you want:

Part One covers the three main reasons that we struggle to know what we want.

Part Two lays the foundations and introduces your first decision, the one that affects all the others.

Part Three looks at why it is so hard to know our own mind and what to do about it.

Part Four will take you step by step through a series of exercises to discover your deepest longings. After each step is a practical exercise to help you discover what you want and a deeper explanation for those who want to use these tips with others.

Part Five suggests a way to start having what you want.

Part Six summarises the twelve rules for knowing what you want.

Part Seven points out some common problems with keeping this going and gives you tips to overcome them.

Part Eight looks at two useful ways of maintaining the habit of knowing your own mind.

Part Nine shows you how to use your holiday to set successful goals.

Part Ten looks at the most frequently asked questions about knowing what you want.

And we end with some references and ideas for further help.

In the next section I explain how to get the best from this book.

How To Use This Book

Did you know that 50% of people who buy a book like this never get beyond Chapter One?

If you want to get the very best from your time with this book, use the hints below to help you make the most of it.

Let's start with what's included. In this book you'll find:

- Explanations for why it is so hard to know what you want.

- 12 easy steps to follow that will teach you how to know what you want.

- Graduated exercises that build the skill of knowing your own mind.

- Advice for those days when you are stumped.

- And details of the free bonus that comes with the book

Probably the best way to use this material is to play. Dip in. Read the suggestions. Do all the exercises – or just one. You will surprise yourself how clear and firm your ideas become. The future that looked blank and empty will begin to fill up with ideas, goals, and desires. As you complete each exercise you'll acquire skills you can use every day and with others.

Plan To Know What You Want

Learning to know what you want involves everything you have got. Your body, your mind, your senses and your full attention.

Why not plan for this? Make a deliberate plan to give this your full attention. Unplug yourself from the daily hassle, turn your phone off, find somewhere nice to go while you complete the exercises. Buy a special book to write in and treat yourself to a new pen.

(Of course you may not have a borderline stationery fetish like me; but whatever helps!)

You will want to dream, to ponder, to stare off into the distance. Find some undistracted time where it is OK to do this. Adopt a coffee shop, rediscover the library, use the down time while your kids do sports. And as you give it your attention, the answers will begin to reveal themselves to you.

The Power Of Writing

Working through these exercises is going to generate a lot of new thinking, ideas, suggestions and plans. *Write it all down.* Much later we'll look at how to sort through all your thoughts but for now take the time to write it all down. There is something about writing down your thoughts that enables you to see them more clearly.

If it helps, find a buddy to work through the exercises with and encourage each other on the journey.

If writing is a struggle, find a way of preserving what you think so that you can see it or hear it again – use a voice recorder, video yourself speaking through the exercises, make mindmaps – find some way of preserving the thoughts ideas and suggestions that will pop up as you work through the chapters.

If you can, write it down. Reading through the exercises is not the same. To get the most impact (and the most value), download your free **'First Know Journal'** (below) and use that.

Lay The Foundations

The earlier exercises lay foundations for the later techniques. The way to get the most value from this book is to work through Parts One to Three and make sure you do Steps One to Four in Part Four in that order. After that you can dip in and out to suit yourself or work through the rest in order. This will ensure you develop good habits for knowing what you want.

Short Of Time? Use Quick Reads

At the end of every chapter you will find a quick read section which you can refer back to quickly or skim if you are short of time. These notes explain the thinking behind the exercises. Read these if you want to help others know what they want.

Each Quick Read ends with a Key Points summary.

Grab Your Free Bonus

Visit *www.firstknowwhatyouwant.com* to download your free extras. Get your free **'First Know Journal'** – a companion workbook with more space to complete the exercises. You can print it as many times as you want or share with friends. We'll also send you a story. Follow the adventures of Mike Johnson, a harassed middle manager as he works with his coach to discover what he wants.

You'll also find links to our recommended reading and some of our favourite resources for making up your mind.

And One Other Thing...

Treat this as a workbook and a toolkit, write on it, scribble across it, doodle, cross things out and so on.

Please make it yours. I really want you to be clear about what you want and so find the motivation to go and get it.

Ready to play?

Part 1: First, Know What You Want

This book is about how to know what you want. Alone among the animals, we can make up our mind and choose a path or direction. But it's not easy to choose and we use all sorts of behaviour to avoid having to make that choice.

Everything in life that you haven't done yet or isn't yet the way you want it to be, boils down to one of two problems:

- You know what you want but you don't know how to get it.

- You don't yet know what you want.

This book is a toolkit to help you with the second problem – being clear about what you want.

Self-Help Doesn't Help

Have you read any of those self help books? Or listened to the self help gurus. They all say one thing – to have a better life, you must set goals. Fine, but what if you don't know what you want or can't decide among all the choices you have?

Let's face it, you could all do almost anything. Your choices are practically infinite – and that's the problem, there's too much choice. It's overwhelming – and then there's all the other stuff that crowds in to muddy the view – stuff like fear, worries, responsibilities and pressures on time etc.

How can you start moving forward in your life if you don't know where to go?

It seems like the shelves of our bookshops are groaning with ways of helping you achieve your goals, find the partner of your dreams, get better relationships, lose weight, change career etc, but they all miss one obvious truth.

If you ask most people what they want, they don't know. Why is this? Surely it should be easy. You just ask yourself what you want, make a decision and do it. For a tiny minority of people this is what happens. They were born knowing what they wanted and it's never been a problem.

For most people though, being clear about what they want, enough to pursue it, is a distant dream. In fact if you ask them they may avoid the question or become angry with you.

This book has one simple idea. Before you can set any goals for yourself you have to know, for certain, what you want. And until you do, you will stay stuck right where you are.

Who Should Read This? Who Is This For?

The steps in this programme can help anybody who is struggling to get clear on what they want.

- People with physical challenges around weight and health who want to do something different.

- Managers who want to help their teams think differently and come up with new ideas.

- Hard working people stuck in jobs or careers that no longer fulfill them.

- People wrestling with a change of life, new job, new relationships, new challenges.

- Students wanting to decide what to do with their future.

- Men and women in their first job, wanting a change but not knowing where to go.

If you are a highly motivated person who regularly sets goals and achieves them, then this is not for you. Buy it for a friend, work colleague or family member who could do with some of the clarity you already have. There is plenty here that will help them.

If you're a professional, racking your brains for effective ways to help your clients know their own minds and become self determined then, again, there are many tools here which might sit comfortably in your toolbox.

What Is Your Real Experience Of Trying To Know What You Want?

Not knowing what you want causes real pain.

I've got used to being interrupted in the middle of my presentation by people who want to tell the whole group that they'd finally figured it out. I still remember one lady stopping me: *"After 30 years, I finally know what I should be doing."* Are you going to wait this long?

What is your real experience of trying to know what you want?

- You know you can do loads of things but you don't know which one to do.

- You feel that you don't stick at anything.

- When your survey all your possibilities you feel neutral about them all.

- You know that you are capable of doing a great many things but none of them stand out as the one thing.

- Your passion for new things has cooled or been blunted because of past failures.

- You know yourself too well to be fooled by a little simple visioning. You've set goals before and then failed to stick to them.

- You have a fondness for sabotaging yourself.

- You look around at the values of the world, the things you are supposed to want, and you find them hollow. So you do nothing instead of creating an alternative.

- You're cut down, overwhelmed and worn out, worn down by the busyness of life.

- You have fought yourself before and lost. You do not relish another fight.

- You despair and wish someone would appear with the answer.

That's pretty painful. It would be so much easier if an angel could appear with a big sign saying "Go here", "Do this" but they won't. We have to find a way of figuring this out. And there's more...

They Are Looking For You

Advertisers are on the lookout for people like you. So are politicians and TV producers. They are looking for compliant, passive people who have no clear agenda and long for someone to tell them what to do. They want you to spend your life following *their* agenda, buying their products and watching the crap they feed you.

How long though? How long can you ignore your inner call that there has to be something more for you?

What You'll Learn From Reading This Book

Follow every step of this programme and long before you reach the end you will have rediscovered the skill of knowing what you want. You'll be able to decide what you want, take the right action and get the result.

Follow these steps and you'll:

- Make small decisions much faster.
- Make big decisions more easily.
- Untangle what you want from how you feel.
- Know what you want in every situation.
- Know your own mind more clearly.
- Develop original thinking.
- Work out what is important to you.
- Know how to use what you don't want.
- Set goals and achieve them, every time.
- Help family, friends and colleagues know what they want.

- Improve time management and productivity.

- Get back in touch with your senses.

- Look back on a life lived the way you wanted it.

- Remove daily irritants from your life.

- Reduce clutter and improve your physical surroundings.

- Distinguish fantasy from dreams and make your dreams come true.

- Find your inner compass and learn to follow it.

- Know what to do when completely stumped.

- Avoid self-sabotage and discouragement.

- Develop the habit of quickly knowing what want in any situation.

- Unlock your motivation to move your life in the direction of what you want.

- Gain a kitbag of tools, techniques and strategies to help colleagues, clients, family and friends to discover what they want.

- If you are a parent you will be able to help your children pick a direction.

- If you are a counsellor, coach or other professional you will be able to help your clients discover what they want.

- If you manage others you will pick up a number of techniques to unlock their motivation.

How A Fly Can Help You

Have you ever seen a fly trying to get through a window? It can see the light but when it flies towards it – bang! – it runs straight into an invisible barrier. The harder it tries the more it hurts itself.

So what does it do? Let's say it consults a nearby self-help book that recommends setting challenging goals.

Having done that, it tries again and – bang! – straight into an invisible barrier. So off it goes to a motivational talk, three hours of cheerleading followed by a fire-walk. Pumped up, ready to go for it, full of the joys of clarity and purpose and **bang**! Straight into an invisible barrier. No matter how hard it tries it cannot get past the thing that's stopping it getting to the light.

What is a fly to do? Try even harder?

Nope, that way lies death.

How about this? Step back gently and take a look at the bigger picture. Do that and you will see a little gap which you can fly through with no effort at all. If you've been wrestling with the problem of knowing what you want and you've tried everything then relax. There is no trying here. All we are going to do is take a step or two back and see if we can find you a gap.

It's Actually About Attention

Figuring out what you want is not your problem. You already know that. The real problem is *attention* and that's what this is all about – where your attention is now and where it could be. It's all about paying attention.

Let me explain. Somebody once told me: if you don't pay with attention you pay with pain. What kind of pain? The pain of not being clear on what you want, the pain of frustration and the sense of unease it causes. You have this pain because you are doing something else with your attention. And I think you know this, don't you? You know that if you paid attention, you could know what you wanted. It's just that your attention is somewhere else. Curious isn't it? What have you allowed to be more important than knowing your own mind?

As you work through the exercises you'll gain a toolkit to help you bring your attention to bear on the problem of figuring out what you want. I promise you, if you bring your attention here, then what you want will reveal itself, and a way will open that feels right. You're going to have to pay attention though, which means before we go any further we have got to talk about the myth of multi-tasking.

The Myth Of Multitasking

Multitasking is a myth. We are just not capable of it. I know the old joke that men can only do one thing at a time, while women manage several but brain research shows that none of us are capable of multitasking. We are simply not built that way.

Hold on, you might be saying. Not only have I seen people multitasking, I've done it myself.

Really?

Watch closely next time you see someone multitasking. Watch yourself closely next time you think you are multitasking. You'll notice that what you're actually doing is using very thin slices of attention. You're switching rapidly from thing to thing, with your brain thrashing around like a caught fish. Whilst you can set more than one plate spinning at a time, you can only pay attention to one of them at a time.

It's family meal time. You are in the kitchen. You are stirring a pot which has 100% of your attention for a second or two. Your daughter asks a question, you switch attention, she has 100% until the oven timer goes off, then that gets 100% until the phone rings and you answer but even as you answer, your attention switches back to the pot which is near to boiling. *"Mummy?"* There it goes again.

Some people are good at this kind of rapid context switching but being good at it does not make this an efficient process. It means that almost nothing gets your sustained, focused, attention. And that attention is what it takes to make a real difference to a problem or to make a partner, child or friend feel wanted. Research shows that a programmer, deep in code, takes nearly 11 minutes to re-enter that focused, attentive state after an interruption. Imagine the effect of being constantly interrupted – nothing of any quality gets done.

In fact, the kind of rapid attention switching that we call multitasking is a form of defensive behaviour, a reaction to an unparalleled onslaught of distraction and information. Never before have we faced so many choices with so little training on how to handle them. This kind of frantic switching from thing to thing only leaves you frazzled and with the puzzled sense that you have been doing everything but have actually done nothing.

Whatever you are doing with your attention at the moment, as you read this book, you will find yourself increasingly paying attention to what you want on a whole number of levels – if you are willing to bring all of your attention here for a while.

Whatever you do and wherever you do it, I hope you'll rediscover the power of bringing all your attention to bear on one thing for more than a micro second.

Part 2: Laying The Foundations

Before we look in detail at what stops us knowing what we want, we need to lay some good foundations. There's a decision you need to make and an attitude you could adopt to help you.

Your First Decision

In your world there are people who know what they want. We call them charismatic because their amazing clarity beguiles and charms us. In a confused world, such single-minded focus is rare and alluring. They have a purpose, a clear plan and their own agenda. **Unless you are the same, you will end up working for one of these people.**

Without an agenda of your own you will spend your life fulfilling someone else's agenda. Jesus once described people as *sheep, looking for a shepherd* and he wasn't far wrong. Your boss, government, family or culture all have an agenda and they are looking for mild, confused and passive people to work on it. If this isn't OK with you, you owe it to yourself to know your own mind.

Good News If You Don't Know What You Want

The good news is, it can be done. No matter what your previous experience, it is completely possible for you to know what you want *and* discover the motivation to go and get whatever it is.

There's something about this that has your attention, isn't there? I don't know what it is. It might be a specific area of your life where you are trying to know what you want. It might be that general sense that you could be doing more with yourself; if only you could get clear on what it is that you want. You may feel or long for this kind of clarity because you believe that, once you are clear about it, you can commit to a firm direction.

Lying underneath this though is an unspoken decision. Before you can start to know what you want, you have to do something else. There is a decision you need to make before you can make all the other decisions.

Your First Decision

Whatever it is that keeps nagging at you, it's worth taking a moment to consider the bigger decision, the unspoken one, the first decision *before* you can go on to know what you want. And it's this…

Have you decided that you actually want to know what you want?

I know it seems a strange question. Of course you do, but stay with me for a moment.

Why Make This First Decision?

Researchers in creativity have found that the single biggest thing that helps people become more creative is when they *decide* to become more creative. There is something about making this decision that either sparks more creativity or makes it OK for you to discover and express your creativity.

In the same way, **now is the time to *decide* that you want to know what you want.**

Why? Because making this decision will support you through the rest of these exercises. Without it, there is a chance you could sabotage your own efforts.

I've got some questions for you.

Making Your First Decision

- How do you know that you want to know what you want?

- How would you convince a good friend that you have made a firm decision to figure this out?

The first decision you need to make is that nothing is going to stop you from deciding what you want, no matter how difficult this seems or how many times you may have failed in the past. How would you convince a good friend of this? Once you are clear about this, have a go at the questions below.

What's in it for you to know what you want? What will you gain?

Make a list. For example, your list might look like this:

- *I'll gain a sense of direction.*

- *I'll know what to do about my future career.*

- *I'll be able to make future decisions more quickly.*

What will you have to lose or give up or stop once you know what you want?

If you truly knew what you wanted, what would you have to leave behind or lose? Make another list. For example:

- *I'll lose a big reason for not doing anything.*

- *And I suppose if I knew, I'd lose all those long conversations with friends when I keep going over what I don't know.*

- *Oh I can see that I might, in truth, lose some choices by coming to a firm decision.*

- *And if I'm honest I'm a bit scared of finding out what I want because it might mean big changes for me so I suppose I'll lose some comfort.*

What will happen if you don't know what you want?

If nothing changes for you, write down what will happen.

- *I'll stay stuck and I'll end my life standing in a bar telling stories of what I could have done.*

What won't happen if you don't know what you want?

- *I won't have to make any changes in my life. Everything will be pretty much the same.*

These questions help you to look at the problem from all sides. It is not enough just to think about what something new will bring you. You know that because you have been resisting figuring out what you want, you must have a strong reason for this. Asking these questions helps you to see round the problem:

'What will you gain?' is straightforward.

'What will you lose?' may reveal the thing that is preventing you figuring it all out for yourself.

'What will happen if you don't figure it out?'

This question gets you to ponder the consequences of carrying on like this and *'What won't happen if you don't?'* gets you to ponder the downside of the possible gains.

Overleaf, you'll find these questions with space to make your own notes and although you don't have to write the answers down it will make a big difference if you do. Why not find a quiet corner and give them your full attention?

Make This Decision First Or Nothing Else Will Work

There is no way of softening this. Until you have made this first decision it is pointless to continue because nothing else I'm going to suggest will work. Decide for yourself first, that you *want* to know what you want and second, that you *will* know what you want.

I can't help you unless you are totally clear about this.

Exercise: Making Your First Decision

Answer these questions as honestly as you can.

Are you ready to know what you want?

- How do you know that you do want to know what you want?

- How would you convince a good friend that you've made a firm decision to know what you want?

- What's in it for you to know what you want? What will you gain?

- What will you have to lose or give up or stop, once you know what you want?

- What will happen if you don't know what you want?

- What won't happen if you don't know what you want?

Now make a commitment to the process by signing below:

I have decided that I will know what I want. I will give myself every possible assistance to know what I want. And nothing will stop me.

Name:	
Date:	

Who Drives Your Bus?

Before moving on to look at the reasons why it is so hard to make up our mind about what we want, let's take a look at an attitude and approach that can help you.

If your life were a bus, who is driving?

Most people are passengers. To find out why, we need to go back to a story as old as the earth itself. Sometimes the oldest stories contain the most compelling truths. This one cuts right to the heart of this problem of knowing what we want for ourselves and our lives.

It Wasn't Me

Imagine paradise. A fully functioning earth without the bad bits. A perfect climate, abundant food and best of all, no fear. Where animals do not fear or eat each other and they are not afraid of us either. Into this world God puts the first man and woman, giving them a few simple ground rules to follow.

You know the story. Tempted by the desire to be like God they break a rule and it's the next bit of the story that's so insightful about us and about how we struggle to make our lives work for us.

God comes looking for Adam, who is hiding. They get into a conversation about what happened and what does Adam do? Yep, he blames someone else. In fact he manages to try and make it God's fault: 'It was that woman who *you* put here.' God turns to the woman, who promptly blames the snake.

Adam managed to blame his wife *and* God for putting her in the garden, Eve blamed the serpent and nobody took responsibility. And we've been doing it ever since. We are past masters at shifting any kind of blame or responsibility for our own choices away from ourselves.

Are You A Driver Or A Passenger?

Are you a driver or a passenger in the bus of your life?

It's easy to tell if someone is a driver or a passenger. Listen and you'll hear passengers sitting at the back of their bus complaining about where their bus is going. Not only do they complain but they hold someone or something else responsible for where the bus ends up.

Some blame their past: *What happened in my past means I can't or I'm not responsible.*

Some blame their parents, their partner, their boss.

Some use science to shift responsibility: *It's not my fault I'm rude, I've got a gene that makes me rude.*

Some blame the weather: *I'm miserable because it's raining.*

Some are a bit more creative or take a more spiritual approach. They blame the universe, karma, God or their stars.

Since the beginning of time we've been avoiding responsibility for our choices and our actions, looking outside ourselves for the cause of wherever we are now.

We're Still Doing It

Many of us are still doing what Adam and Eve did. Although with more of us around, it's even worse. Passengers get together with other passengers and remind each other that nothing is their fault: *Don't worry, no one can lose weight over 40, you're just big boned!*

You'll hear passengers say things like *Life's a bitch and then you die* or *Same shit, different day* because they believe life is something that happens to you and there is nothing you can do about it. *Pass*engers are *pass*ive, they act like victims and have a victim mentality. And victims need someone to blame.

Become A Driver To Know What You Want

Can you see how this would get in the way of figuring out what you want?

If you think and act like a passenger you probably don't believe that having what you want is possible, so you avoid thinking about it.

The cure is beginning to think and act like a driver. I'd like you to practise imagining that your life is a bus and you are in the drivers seat.

Think about where you are in life right now, the state of your finances, your happiness, your job, your relationships, the amount of fun you have and say to yourself: *I'm where I am right now because I drove my bus right here.*

Immediately you may spring to your own defence. This is not fair. In fact you're thinking of several things that happened where it wasn't your fault – the blame lies squarely with others.

What you're experiencing, right now, is your inbuilt passenger tendency, a direct line back to Adam or Eve, the ancient habit of putting responsibility outside of ourselves. Let's break it down in some detail.

Learn To Take Responsibility, Not Blame

First, it's not about blame. Blame is a feeling, an emotional response, like guilt. Taking responsibility creates an uncomfortable feeling, so we avoid anything that might make us feel that way. Passengers do not want to be blamed so they look to shift the feeling somewhere else. It's safer, and it feels nicer, to blame others or your circumstances or your past. This leaves you stuck. If you are just a victim of circumstance how could you possibly change your life? You have to find a way of taking responsibility without feeling blamed.

How?

One way is to think of your results so far as just data.

- *I made these choices and this happened.*

- *If I make different choices, different things will happen.*

It's not about blame (which leaves you stuck). It's about taking responsibility.

What drivers do is recognise the part they played in what happened and think about what else they could do. A driver knows...

- they can always choose their reaction
- they can always choose where to focus
- they can always choose their next action
- and if they have driven their bus somewhere they don't like, they can always drive it somewhere else

You can only do this if you are willing to take 100% responsibility for the choices, reactions, focus and actions that brought you to where you are now. This is neither nice nor comfortable but it is powerful. After all, if you drove your bus here then you can pretty much drive wherever you want.

And notice that while passengers are figuring out who to blame or where to put the blame, the drivers are busy driving somewhere else. Passengers wonder what happened and why? Drivers make things happen.

How Does All Of This Help Me Know What I Want?

Taking responsibility for what happens in your life is the missing piece, the clue that will finally help you to know what you want.

It's going to take practice though. Start by looking at everything you have and see if you can trace back the choices, focus, reactions and actions that led you here. And in particular I want you to look at things that you are perhaps not totally happy with and see if you can take 100% responsibility without falling into blaming yourself. Blame makes you feel bad and rarely leads to action. Taking responsibility helps you treat the results you get as data and helps you think about alternative actions.

When You Start Driving, People Will Notice

The other thing I want you to listen for is **passenger language** in your colleagues, friends and family. Listen and watch for it, too, in the things you read and see. You'll be astonished how widespread it is – from executives attributing their failure to government policy, to individuals sidestepping their choices because someone didn't give them something.

Listen for people shifting the responsibility for their choices, their actions, their reactions to some external cause.

Once you train your ear to this, it's very tempting to point it out to people. Be careful because sharing it may not make you popular. The passenger mentality is deeply held and no one will thank you for challenging it. Far better to practise being able to spot yourself doing it first. When you start driving, people will notice soon enough.

My other tip is **start small**. Let's say you open your middle desk drawer and notice all the mess in there. Your internal dialogue starts up:

It's not my fault, I have so much work to do, I'm so stressed, they expect too much of me round here, I never get time to clear up... and so on.

All of a sudden you have gone from an untidy drawer to reinforcing your view of yourself as a put upon victim of circumstance and greedy bosses. That's what I mean by listen out for passenger talk. Take a driver's view of it:

OK it's a mess. I don't have time to get to it now. I'm OK with leaving it as a mess for now or I'm going to take everything out of it at lunchtime and put it straight.

Can you feel how much lighter this is, can you hear the difference in the approaches, it even looks different doesn't it?

Do You Create Results Or Reasons?

Good. Now let's take it one step further. Have you ever been in the position of asking someone else to do something for you?

If you have, then you'll know that you usually get one of two things, either they do it (you get a result) or they don't do it (and you get a reason). What kind of person are you? Are you the kind that generally creates results or do you generally create reasons?

A results person? Are you sure? Perhaps you can remember spending an entire meeting brainstorming a list of reasons why something had not been done. Or preparing your excuses in advance for a missed deadline?

Reasons is just a polite word for *excuses* and excuses often have to do with blaming something or someone else for the lack of results. *Sorry I'm late, it was the traffic, If only my boss was more flexible / friendly / open...* and so on.

If you're looking to make a significant difference to your future direction, one thing you can do right now is make a decision to become a results person.

How To Become A Results Person

How? **Get rid of all your reasons.** Stop inventing them and stop using them. Without reasons the only things that's left will be results. When you say yes, mean yes. When you make a promise, keep it. Keep your eye firmly on your results.

How To Spot A Reason

Learn to spot the appearance of a reason because it is so damaging to your results. Did you know there is a big clue that tells you when you are going to get a reason instead of a result? It's a three letter word, a dead giveaway, hear this word and you know there will be a reason coming along soon.

It's the word TRY. When you hear this word you know that a reason is coming. Let me give you an example from home.

My wife is going out for the evening and just before she leaves she asks me to tidy up the kitchen and wash up while she's out.

Me: *I'll try.*

What do you think will really happen? By promising to *try* I have avoided an absolute commitment and I'm probably not going to do it.

You can guess the rest. When she comes back some hours later the place is still a tip. She's understandably upset and feels let down but, luckily for me, I have a good defence.

I tried (just what I promised) *but this happened and that happened.*

I rehearse my list of reasons secure in the knowledge that they let me off the hook.

Does any of this sound familiar?

If you want to give yourself the power to create all the results you want (and who doesn't?) then start by banning the word *try* from your daily life and work. A results person does things or does not do them while a reasons person tries things then invents excuses to cover themselves. Actually, it's impossible to try to do things.

Try And Stand Up

And in case you are in any doubt, try and stand up.

You can sit down now. Look again at what I asked you to do. *Try* and stand up now. You can't can you? It's impossible because the state of *trying* to do something does not exist. You are either standing or you're not. Nothing in between.

For most situations *trying* something is a virtual guarantee of not doing it.

Every time you use the word *try* you are setting yourself up to create reasons. Promise yourself that from now on you will either do things or not do them – no more trying. And that includes figuring out what you want. No more *trying* to know what you want, you are either going to do it or you're not going to do it, aren't you?

Take a week to practise being a driver and then we'll get started on helping you know what you want.

(I wonder what would have happened if the first man had said, *Yes, it was me, I did it, it was wrong and I'm sorry?* We might still be in Eden now.)

Quick Read: Who Drives Your Bus?

In the end, it always comes down to this – who is driving your bus? I met a researcher the other day who told me that the most common characteristic of successful people is that they are 'goal-directed', in other words in any given situation they will look for what to do next and do it. You can only do this if at least some part of you believes that you can influence your own situation or, in my language, if you are a Driver.

People who think like a Driver find it much easier to get to know what they want and they also find it easier to discover the motivation to go and get it, once they have figured it out. Passengers, on the whole, don't.

Passengers:

- take little responsibility for results.
- act as if they're a victim of circumstance.
- believe they have no choice over the behaviour they are exhibiting right now.
- may blame their history.
- may blame others, they say things like, *They made me.*
- may blame their ancestors – *It's bad karma.*
- may use a scientific excuse – *I have a gene that makes me rude.*
- view life as fixed and their results as inevitable.
- take comfort from knowing that since they have so little influence they cannot be blamed for their results.
- coming to a training event or business meeting will blame the room, the trainer or the other people or even fate/karma for their experience.
- can often be found asking themselves, *Why is this happening?*
- will rehearse reasons (excuses) why things did not happen. Reasons will dominate their conversation.

You see the passenger mentality in a man or woman who takes the role of *victim* in their life. The core belief is that they have no choice. To be a good passenger you must constantly deny two things:

- your own role in creating your circumstances.
- your own power to change your circumstances.

Drivers:

- take full responsibility for the results they see in their lives.

- are able to choose their emotional reaction to events and circumstances.

- believe they always have a choice so they are able to generate lots of new options for themselves.

- are willing to face the discomfort of owning up to their own role in creating situations.

- understand that any outside force in their lives is only influential insofar as they let it influence their next choice.

- understand that another person (boss, etc.) is only an influence in their life insofar as they let them.

- coming to a training event or business meeting know that no matter how bad or how good things get, they can always get the result they want. Why? Because they are responsible for getting it and they know that with enough flexibility they can get anything.

- will frequently ask themselves, *How can I make a change to change this situation?*

- will use tend to use **results based** language. You won't hear excuses from them. Drivers will talk about where they are going and what they are doing – the **results** they want.

To be an effective driver you must:

- act as if your choices create your circumstances – whatever they are.

- act as if you have the power to change your situation by making different choices.

On the whole it's easier to know what you want if you operate as a Driver rather than a Passenger.

A World Full Of Passengers

Many of us are quite happy to sit back in the passenger seat while someone else drives the bus – parents, partners, colleagues, our boss, the government. Every so often we may look out of the window and wistfully imagine going somewhere else, but we pretty much act as passengers in our own life.

The exercises in Part Four will help you to begin to figure it out and, just as important, are a set of tools you can use to help others figure it out too.

And if you want to make this work for you then start by making a commitment to yourself that you will hop into the driver's seat of your bus and take responsibility for where it goes.

Of course, it's easy for me to write this. How do you actually start driving your bus – especially if you've been a passenger for a while?

The Easy Way To Become A Driver

Take a good look at your life – weight, finances, relationships, job, business , etc., and ask yourself, *What is my role in creating this?*

Because, after all, if you are going to drive your bus then you need to act as if you created it all.

For all the stuff you like and want more of, ask yourself, *How can I create more of this?*

For all the stuff you don't like and want less of, ask yourself, *How can I create something different?*

What Is Your Role In Creating This?

Now act. Do more of the things that will create what you want. Stop or do less of the things that create the results you don't like. The moment you feel yourself going passive, ceding control of your results to parents, partners, colleagues, bosses or even political institutions, then go right back to the beginning: *What is my role in creating this?*

I don't know whether we do create all the results in our lives but I do know that by acting as if we do, we greatly increase our ability to change all our results. Perhaps the best guidance of all comes from CS Lewis: *Pray as if it all depended on God and work as if it all depended on you.*

Do your bit with everything you've got, let the rest go, and it becomes much easier to know where you want to go. Just as if you were driving your own bus.

Part 3: Why Is It So Hard To Know What We Want?

It should be easy, shouldn't it? So why don't we know what we want? And it's not just you. Most people, apart from a small minority, seem to be stuck in this limbo of doing OK but thinking there might be something else, although they haven't much of an idea what. What's going on?

I think there are three major reasons that we don't know what we want:

- We lack practice.

- We've trained ourselves to look the wrong way.

- When we do think about it we get scared and overwhelmed.

Before I go on though, remember that your first big decision is that you are going to figure this out. You're committed to making that true for yourself.

Remember too that all of this becomes a lot easier if you are willing to act like a driver, to take responsibility for what you create in your life and how you react to what shows up. Acting as if you create your own results will help, but it is not the whole story.

There are still some things that mean it is hard for us to make up our mind about what we want. Let's go through them one by one:

Reason 1: We Lack Practice

Why don't we know what we want? Sometimes its simple. We just lack the practice, we have weak decision making muscles. If you're an averagely nice person who never offends anyone, you probably just go with the flow. You generally get along with colleagues and friends. You don't make a fuss because it's easier not to and you probably look askance at people who do.

Because of this you are simply not used to deciding what you want and holding out for it. You rarely make that kind of decision. Your boss decides when you arrive at work and when you leave, how long your lunch should be and how much holiday you can have (and when). Your spouse organises your social life (and your socks). You fit in, watching the same TV, doing what others do. Even the way you dress or the kind of car you drive helps you to fit in and feel safe, not too different. Believe me, you lack practice in deciding what you want.

It's no wonder, is it, that when it comes to the bigger issues in life we have no experience to fall back on. **We've not practiced the skill enough to use it when we need it.**

Hang on a minute though. *I admit I might live on autopilot a bit but isn't that just politeness? You can't go around making a fuss about what you want the whole time, can you?*

The Solution For Your Lack Of Practice

Let's see. If we lack practice deciding what we want then the solution is pretty obvious. You have to practise. Think about a pianist doing scales or a footballer rehearsing moves. You have to go right back to the beginning, to the smallest parts of your life and practise deciding what you want. We'll talk more about how to set up this practice later but why? Why is this so important?

All Those Broken Agreements Mean
You've Lost Faith In Yourself

This lack of practice in making your own decisions gets compounded because you have been let down so many times. Imagine a friend of yours who keeps promising to meet you for lunch but never shows and worse, keeps coming up with the most lame excuses that you can hardly believe: *My back was aching today. The cat was sick so I couldn't come. I got distracted by this TV programme and before I knew it the time had gone.*

How would you feel about this person? Annoyed? Let down? That they weren't a real friend?

Guess who you have been letting down? That's right. Imagine a life littered with broken promises, full of intentions that never went anywhere and ideas that never got further than fantasy. Imagine that lot hanging round your neck. No wonder you feel confused. You're feeling let down and probably slightly angry.

Lack of practice has deprived you of the skill of knowing what you want. Let's look at the second reason.

Reason 2: We've Trained Ourselves To Look The Wrong Way

Imagine this. An eight year old boy is playing in the garden one day when he takes a fresh look at the garden wall. It might be fun to walk along the top.

Imagine what I could see, It would be like flying.

He notices a way up to the top of the wall that he never saw before. It's an effort but there he is walking along the top of the wall enjoying the view with this arms spread, pretending to fly. It's wonderful.

His mother, glancing out the window, shrieks in horror and rushes out into the garden yelling at the top of her voice: *Don't move. Stay where you are. Get down from there. How did you get up there? You'll fall off and kill yourself. Don't ever do that again.*

Faced with this wail of contradictory advice and admonishment, the full emotional force of a mother in distress, he begins to realise, perhaps for the first time, that he could indeed be killed, it is dangerous and he will fall off.

Suddenly he is no longer stable, he feels unsteady and vulnerable. He gets down. He sees clearly what he does not want to happen and it stays with him.

Weren't you scared? Mum asks. He realises that he should have been scared, that it would please her if he was scared. So he gets scared.

From now on, whenever he looks at the wall a strong, negative image of the consequences comes to him. A bit of him still wants to be up on the wall but now it feels nasty. He's confused. He learns to ignore what he wants. He knows clearly what he does not want and he is afraid of it.

How Your Parents Trained You
To Look The Wrong Way

Throughout our childhood our parents, motivated by love and care for our safety, reinforce over and over again the negative consequences of taking action.

Don't run across the road without looking, you'll be killed.

We get good at focusing on the negative, the downside, the consequences. So now when we cross the road we are not thinking, *How can I get to the other side safely?* Instead we are thinking, *I've got to watch out in case I get killed, and get this done as quickly as possible.* In their love, our parents continually reinforce the negative, what you don't want, what is wrong.

Don't cross the road. Don't make a risky decision. Don't skip your homework.

The reinforcement is strong, emotional and repeated. **Is it any wonder that we learn to pay attention only to what we don't want or are afraid of?**

In this way our ability to understand our enjoyable desires is squashed by years of practice at knowing, clearly, what we do not want. The odd inkling of something we actually do want is feeble and soon drifts away.

Looking The Wrong Way

Simply put, we look the wrong way. I meet few people who can tell me clearly what they want but almost everyone I meet knows, clearly, what they do not want. For some people, talking about what they don't like, don't want and didn't enjoy makes up a large part of their conversation.

How was your holiday?

OK but the flight was late, we got locked out of the hotel and I got food poisoning. They didn't have any English papers.

Can you hear it? A complete focus on the downside, the negative, what went wrong or what could go wrong.

The Second Most Powerful
Question In The World

There is no point asking these people what they want. This is why most goal setting schemes and initiatives fail or only appeal to people who are already motivated. How can you understand what you want when most of your focus is somewhere else?

It's like getting in the car in the morning and working out your route to work by a process of elimination: I don't want to go to Scotland, not France today, not to the cinema etc.

Eventually you will end up at work but the process is long, slow and boring.

This is how millions run their lives. They have a clear and definite focus on what they **don't want** but little idea of what they **do want**. They have their attention firmly on the rear view mirror and live by moving away from things that they don't like. *Nope, I don't like this job. Nope, this relationship hasn't worked.*

What they need to do is obvious isn't it? They need to focus on what they want. The problem is that just because it is obvious doesn't make it easy to do, does it? Otherwise we would all know what we wanted and be moving towards it.

The easiest way to get to work is to sit in your car and say to yourself: *I want to go to...*

Engage the gears and go. But if you've spent your whole life steering by the rear view mirror and working out things by trying them, deciding you don't like or don't want them and then having a go at something else, this switch of focus is too much of a stretch. There is an easier way.

If you know what you don't want then you need to ask yourself the second most powerful question in the world.

What is it? More on that later. For the moment, though, let's look at the third reason that we find it hard to know what we want.

Reason 3: When We Think About It We Get Scared And Overwhelmed

The third major reason that we do not know what we want is our fear of what might happen if we did. Along with this comes the sheer overwhelm of making choices when there are so many things we could want.

Struggling to know what you want is a unique problem for recent generations in the richer parts of the world. Our ancestors had no problem working out what to do. Why? Because the answer was right in front of them – they wanted food, shelter, warmth and a mate; getting these was enough to fill their time. We, on the other hand, have money, freedom, time, comfort and more food than we could ever eat. In a way, all the more obvious and easier decisions have been taken care of. So we are free to think about what our lives mean and what they could mean and, perhaps, what they should mean. That's not a simple thing to work out or nor is there a single easy answer.

The other problem is the sheer number of options open to us. Even buying toothpaste these days means coping with six or seven brands providing nearly 50 different choices. It's no wonder that many people just shut down in the face of all this choice and default to what they bought yesterday or grab the first one they recognise.

Unfortunately, doing more of what you did yesterday or grabbing at the first choice you recognise, fails to satisfy that hollow feeling or quiet that voice whispering that there has to be more for you, somewhere and somehow.

A Blank Page Is Scary

Hand me a blank page, tell me I can draw anything I want and I freeze. My mind goes blank. Panic starts. *What if I do it wrong? What if they laugh? Where do I start?*

I'm not alone.

What about you?

If I gave the same page to a child, they would start creating something. They are completely unselfconscious, but pick a teenager or an adult and you get a similar reaction to mine.

A blank future is just as challenging and scary for most of us. What if we do it wrong? What if they laugh? Where do we start?

Other Ways You Scare Yourself

We devise lots of interesting and exciting ways to frighten ourselves out of knowing what we want. Maybe we shy away from exploring other options because we frighten ourselves by thinking about the consequences: *If I did what I wanted I'd have to leave this job, town, relationship.*

We run catastrophic disaster scenarios in which we would have to turn our whole life upside down if we figured out what we wanted. So we don't.

If you've been scaring yourself, it's probably because you are denying to yourself some sort of change that you know you want to make. Remember that being clear about what you feel does not mean that you have to act on those feelings. For example, many people are unhappy in their job and long for more freedom and control over their day. They shy away from facing this because they frighten themselves with the prospect of having to run their own business. Silly, isn't it? There are lots of ways to create more freedom and get more control over your daily life and few of them involve the risk of running your own business. If you never face up to how you feel though, you never get to make these changes.

In reality, most of the changes you are likely to make are actually incremental. It's much more likely to involve small, deliberate steps towards your desires rather than the kind of life-changing, revolutionary fantasies you frighten yourself with.

And the good news is, if you are the kind of person who runs dramatic disaster scenarios in your head, you may just have uncovered a creative side of yourself. An imaginative 'you' who could probably do with coming out to play more often. Maybe the drama is a plea for more creative play?

We Frighten Ourselves With Stereotypes

Another way we frighten ourselves out of understanding our real desires is by the fear of what we might have to become, if we understood what we wanted. The argument goes like this:

If I gave way to what I wanted I would be an actor and since all actors are [poor, crazy, etc.] I don't want to think about what I want.

I think I might want to be a stand up comedian but since presentations make me nervous I'm not going to think about it.

This is just another version of a dramatic disaster scenario. Again, the cure is to realise that running away from a stereotype prevents you considering the smaller, incremental changes that would bring your life much closer to living the way you truly want.

You Can Manage Fear

If some kind of fear, of an imagined possible future, of an imagined possible you, is getting in the way of you knowing what you want, then how do you deal with this? Having practised it for so long, it's unlikely to disappear just because you wish it.

Remember that courageous and brave people are not people who have no fear. A brave person is someone who knows they are afraid but keeps going anyway.

Fear Is Not A Signal

Many of us assume that fear is an intuitive signal to keep away from something but it isn't. It's just your unconscious early warning system flagging up something for attention. Fear is not a red light that tells you something is broken and needs fixing; it is a red light that says: *By the way, did you know this?*

If you see the process of getting clear on what you want as a threat to your stability and wellbeing then your early warning system (fear) will start flashing whenever you go near it.

43

Being brave says: *Yes I know this frightens me but I'm going to look anyway or I've never liked the sound of this but I'm going to ignore the alarm bells and explore it or whenever I think about this I feel nervous but I'm going to push through it anyway.*

Fear is just data. Treat is as such. Your unconscious has alerted you for which you are grateful but you intend to go ahead anyway because you want to/you are curious. This puts you in charge and reminds your fear that it is not the boss here.

When You Face Overwhelming Choices

There are so many things you could do and some of them contradict each other. Some of them cost money you don't have. Faced with this, it's easier to ignore them all. You may have a sense that looking at what you want too closely would open a can of worms. For peace of mind it's easier not to look.

Trouble is, as you know, you haven't got peace of mind otherwise you wouldn't be reading this. What you need is a system. A way of figuring out what you want and managing your choices so they are less overwhelming.

Yep, You'll Contradict Yourself

Absolute clarity about what you want is rare. It's unlikely that you will find one desire that trumps all the others and makes clear to you what you should do. You are much more likely to have a handful of wants which all seem pretty important and some of which contradict each other.

We are complex beings. Ignore those who tell you to set a single big goal because we rarely, if ever, have the luxury of paying attention to just one big goal. I never understand how business people will pay to listen to the 'lessons' from famous sports stars. High achieving sports people operate in such a cosseted, artificial environment that they have little to say to the rest of us about achievement in the real world.

At some point you have to arrange your wants into a hierarchy. To know which one/s you want the most and the key to that, as we'll see later, is to use your personal values to help you.

Key Points: Why Is It So Hard To Know What We Want?

- We lack practice – our decision making muscles are flabby and we coast along with decisions rather than deciding for ourselves.

- We've trained ourselves to look the wrong way – it's become a habit and we are very good at knowing what we don't want.

- When we think about it we get scared and over-whelmed – we know too much, we have too many choices and we let our fear stop us from standing out.

For the next week or two see if you can notice when and where your personal fear signals cut in to stop you. Imagine your fear like an electric fence surrounding how you live. You'll know it when you touch it.

Part 4: How To Discover What You Want

Now that we know more about why it is so hard to discover what we want, it's time to find a solution.

A 12-Step Guide To
Knowing Your Own Mind

Each step builds on the one before and I recommend that you do at least the first four steps in order. The rest you can dip in and out of as you wish. If you've been struggling to make up your mind then give yourself the best chance by doing as many of the exercises as possible.

Here's what you'll learn in each of the twelve steps:

Step 1. Start Small – How to practise the skill of knowing what you want by building your decisionmaking muscles.

Step 2. Start Navigating By Desire – Discover the difference between navigating by mood and navigating by desire.

Step 3. Squash The Bugs To Get Clear About What You Want – Remove that annoying background hum from your life so you can think more clearly.

Step 4. Use What You Don't Want – Use the second most powerful question in the world.

Step 5. Make A Wish List – Turn a long-held fantasy or dream into something that actually happens.

Step 6. Find Your Talents – Let your talents tell you what you want.

Step 7. The Power Of Keeping Score – How keeping score and using scales can accelerate your life.

Step 8. Clear The Decks So Inspiration Can Land – A checklist for that will give you extra energy and clear a space for more inspiration to land.

Step 9. Live Now – Bring your life forward to now.

Step 10. Stop Thinking And Come To Your Senses – Let your senses guide you.

Step 11. Uncover Your Values – Discover the hidden drivers that are most important to you.

Step 12. Follow Your Joy – Excavate the past to provide a signpost for your future.

Turning Theory Into Practice

Each step contains a short exercise that will help you get to the heart of knowing what you want. Doing the exercise, writing down your answers and reflecting on your answers will help you know your own mind.

Quick Reads

For a fast summary of each step just turn to the 'Quick Read' which follows each exercise. These get right to the heart of the technique and contain some extra hints about using these exercises with others.

Key Points

Short of time? At the end of each chapter you'll find the key points. Use these to remind you how to use each exercise.

Download The Workbook

At *www.firstknowwhatyouwant.com* you can find your **'First Know Journal'** to print and use with these exercises. Print it as many times as you like and share with friends.

Step 1: Learn To Start Small

What changes have you begun to notice so far? When you start thinking like a driver **(Part 2)** it's not unusual for you to realise just how far you've let others make decisions for you. The other thing you may notice is just how many times you have broken agreements with yourself.

In the following chapters I'm going to give you lots of different ways to know what you want so that you have loads of choices about how you will decide.

The first solution to knowing what you want is learning to start small. It's simple and easy to do, in fact when I explain it to you, it may seem too easy and you may wonder what the point is but first let me ask you a question...

How Do You Train A Show Jumper?

How do you persuade a horse to jump a six foot fence, against the clock, in a hot crowded arena, with 200 pounds of human on its back?

It seems to me there are two approaches you can use. The first is to set the bar up high, gallop your horse madly towards it and see what happens. If it fails then repeat but this time hit it hard until it is so filled with fear and adrenaline that it crashes over. Then raise the bar again and keep beating the horse to make it jump. Repeat.

The other way is to walk a young horse over a rail that is lying on the ground. Soothe, reassure and make it feel safe. When it is totally comfortable with stepping over, raise it an inch or so. Repeat until the horse is confidently jumping over fences.

You'd be surprised how many people try to use the first approach to know what they want. They charge at the problem and then beat themselves up when the answer does not reveal itself instantly. If you are struggling to know what you want, then raising the bar on yourself is just not going to work. You've probably already tried beating yourself up about it all. (If you haven't, it might be worth giving it a go so that you can convince yourself for all time that it just does not work!)

It's The Second Approach That Works

I'm going with the second approach – starting small and gaining confidence with easy achievements. All I want you to do is learn to work out what you want AND achieve it, by lowering the bar until you can win every time.

The point of starting small is to get you to use the *Decide – Act – Get* cycle. The idea of this exercise is to build your decision making confidence by collecting loads of small wins; so you get used to winning.

The Decide – Act – Get Cycle

First you decide that you want something – a small thing that is easy to get – then you take the required action, then you notice that you have got it. Decide – Act – Get. And you start by picking small, ridiculously small, things so that you teach yourself that you CAN decide what you want, you CAN take the right action and you CAN get it.

Why? Because *not* knowing what you want has become a bad habit you need to break. It goes a bit like this. You struggle to think of something, you half decide that you want it, you don't take the required action and then you get disappointed or angry with yourself that it didn't work. Then you conclude that having what you want is too difficult. And it becomes a habit, pretty soon you are doing it all the time!

By learning to start small we are going to break that habit.

Why Starting Small Will Work For You

For the next week or so I want you to let yourself off the hook, give up any worries or thoughts about the big questions in life, what you should do and where you should go or which choices you should make. Take a week off from all of that and practise lowering the bar until you can decide what you want and get it every single time. I want you to fix your practice so that you win every time and that means lowering the bar until all you are doing is winning. Let me explain…

As you get up ask yourself: *What do I want to wear? The black trousers?* Find them and put them on. Check how you feel. Is this what you want?

Seems trivial and silly doesn't it? And it probably is. And the reason you're doing it is to practice the winning cycle of Deciding, Acting, Getting.

Now, breakfast. *What do I want?* Decide, Act, Get. Suppose you decide cereal but halfway through the bowl you realise that it wasn't actually what you wanted. In fact you are only eating it because it was the last commercial you saw before bed and, in truth, you now realise that you hate this particular cereal. What then? Get up, throw it away and go back to the beginning. *What do I want?* If it's been a long time, then this may take some practice.

Pick five things you will do before you go to bed tonight. This is not the place for stretch goals or outstanding items from your to-do list; the sole purpose of this exercise is to decide you will do them, do them and hit the pillow tonight having done them all. Fix the exercise so that today you win. If you do this properly, for the next seven nights you will hit the pillow having done every single thing you decided to do – if you make them small enough.

So think of something that you are going to do today, something you want, something you want to do. If there is the slightest doubt that you will do it then pick something even smaller until you have something that you have decided to do, that you are willing to act on and that you will notice when you have done it.

Decide then Act then Get

When I first explain this to people in a workshop a few hands will go up complaining that this seems a silly thing to do. They appear aggrieved that they've paid to come to a workshop and were expecting something a bit more sophisticated.

Well, it does seem silly but think about that horse learning to jump and think about you approaching the problem of figuring out what you want. If you drive a horse at a barrier with no training and lack of practice then the horse will quickly come to the conclusion that it can't be done.

It happens to people too, wrestling the problem of figuring out what they want and not resolving it, many simply conclude that it is not possible even though they can see it's possible for others. *I'm just not that kind of person.*

The point of this exercise is to break the cycle and convince yourself completely that you can decide what you want, take action and get it. Think of it as training your decision-making muscles.

Fix Your Practice To Win Every Time

It's important that you lower the bar until you win every time. The key to beginning to know what you want is to practise the skill of figuring out what you want over and over again with small things so that you embed the behaviour of always having an outcome for whatever you do.

You are training yourself for one thing and one thing only; being able to recognise the promptings of your inner compass. As you practise building your decision making muscles it does not matter that the decisions seem trivial. What matters is the constant cycle of **making a decision, acting on your decision and getting the result you intended.**

And as you practise more and more, the promptings of your inner compass will grow louder and louder until you can hear it in any situation.

What do I want from this phone call?

I'm travelling home, what do I want from this journey?

What do I want from this meeting?

What do I want to eat at this meal?

(And if it is not what's in front of you then put it aside and go get what you want). Build the habit of deciding, acting and getting.

Small Means Small

When I suggest picking something small I mean keep reducing the challenge until you can win every time. It's the cycle of picking something, doing it and noticing that you have done it that is important, NOT the size of the goal. We are training your mind with a new pattern here and it's vital that you embed this pattern in yourself over and over again. No broken promises, no half hearted attempts. Pick small goals, shoot and score every single time.

Let's start with something small: *As I leave work I will walk to my car, get in, turn the engine on and start driving.* Yes that small, that simple.

For the next seven days take all those habitual, automatic decisions you make and make them conscious. Decide to do it, do it and notice that you have done it. Begin to walk over those training poles with confidence and authority. You are a person who can decide what you want, take action and achieve it.

And remember, the idea of this is not to start you off making huge changes straight away (although that might happen), the idea of this is to practise being someone who decides what they want and then goes and gets it.

And practise deciding what you want from every experience this week.

Before each meeting: *What do I want from this meeting?*

Before each phone call: *What do I want from this phone call?*

Before each conversation with colleagues: *What do I want from this conversation?*

That's an odd thing isn't it? Thinking about what you want from a conversation with colleagues. Consider this; unless you're just making a noise, you probably have some outcome in mind – you want warmth, connection, friendship, laughter, you want to share a story, you want to feel better by being with them. What is it you want from these conversations? Decide. Act. Get. Teach yourself two important things. First, that you are the kind of person who keeps your word (even to yourself) and secondly that you are the kind of person who can decide what you want, take the right action and get it.

All this low level practice builds muscle memory for the big decisions in life. More on that later.

Man Shall Not Live By Habit Alone

We live on autopilot a lot of the time. Someone asked me once whether I ever work with the blind or deaf, and I do, most of the time! It is amazing how much we cede control of our life to habit or to our boss or our partner so we don't make choices at all. Often we just drift along eating the same food, having same conversations about the same things with the same people all out of habit not out of choice.

From now on I want you to make everything a choice.

Do I want this?

Start, though, with the smallest things.

Won't Making All My Decisions Conscious Slow Everything Down?

All I'm asking you for is a week. Think of it as a week free of concerns about what you want or big decisions, a week spent showing yourself that you can pick something you want, take the right action and then achieve it.

With This Training You Will Surprise People

A word of warning though. Even with this safe level of practice you are going to surprise yourself and may surprise others. Be prepared for this.

It's a day or two later and you've been assiduously practising deciding what you want in the small things. Now you're out to dinner with your partner or perhaps your family. You always have the chicken but as you sit down you're asking *What do I want to eat?* And it comes to you that you would like the fish and you'd like to try a different drink. How will they react, do you think?

Will people be pleased for you? Glad that you are trying new things, encouraged by your creativity? Of course not.

'But you always have the chicken,' they will wail. *'What's wrong?'*

Nope, I'm having the fish, you say, and your conviction surprises you (and them).

Now they are worried. If you are lucky, they will leave it alone and move on to something else. They may not, though, and this will be a test of how firmly you are prepared to stand your ground. Sounds astonishing doesn't it? But wait and see.

Once you begin to be clear about the trivial things in your life, your conviction may surprise you. You may blurt out: *I think...*

I'd like to...

Actually, I've never liked... and I'm not doing it anymore.

You're beginning to have a view, to develop a perspective, to value your own opinion.

This may not be totally comfortable for you and for others but it's a sign of growth. It's also a sign of originality; you are discovering that you have a view, that you know your own mind. The only reassuring thing I can tell you is that this kind of original thinking is charismatic. In the long run you will enjoy this far more than drifting through your life eating chicken because you don't want to offend anybody.

Exercise: Start Small

It's OK to have small goals, especially ones that you are going to achieve easily. Success breeds success. Do not worry if what you want is easily achievable. Achieving your goals, no matter how small they are, will get you into the habit of being someone who is a success at finding out what they want and getting it.

How To Use The Exercise

Start small, with five things you want to achieve before you sleep tonight. Your list might look like this:

- To mow the grass
- To eat well and enjoy my food
- To talk to my partner
- To take the dog for a walk
- To renew the tax for my motorbike

When you are happy and comfortable with your list, do it again, this time for the end of the week, then the end of next week. Repeat for seven days, making them small enough to guarantee a win every time.

Lastly, pick one thing that is small enough for you to guarantee you will achieve it by the end of the month.

BEFORE YOU SLEEP tonight

Make a list of five things you want to achieve BEFORE YOU SLEEP tonight	
1	
2	
3	
4	
5	

Make a list of five things you want to achieve BY THE END OF THE WEEK	
1	
2	
3	
4	
5	

Make a list of five things you want to achieve BY THE END OF NEXT WEEK	
1	
2	
3	
4	
5	

Now one thing you want to achieve BY THE END OF THE MONTH	
1	

Decide – Act – Get

Keep doing this exercise until you get every small thing you have listed here. The most important thing is not what you achieve but that you practise making a decision, taking action and getting the result. Each time you do this, you build the skill of knowing what you want.

Download The Workbook

At *www.firstknowwhatyouwant.com* you can find your **'First Know Journal'** to print and use with these exercises. Print it as many times as you like and share with friends.

Quick Read: Starting Small

This first exercise is all about breaking the bad habit of not knowing what you want.

Pick small things where the answer to the question *What Do I Want?* is easy and within your grasp.

The aim is to notice yourself constantly winning as you practice deciding you want something, taking the right actions and then getting it. As you get good at this you can move onto slightly more stretching decisions but the moment you fail to make it happen, for whatever reason, drop back and pick something easier.

Because you are retraining yourself you need to *fix this exercise so that you always win*. Even though you know you are fixing it and even though you know it's artificial, the practice of being conscious about your decisions will build your confidence. You'll learn that you are the kind of person who is able to decide what they want and take the action needed to achieve it.

The other thing this does is to constantly focus your attention on what *you* want, to break the habit of just going along with others out of boredom or politeness or because it's easier. Making all your decisions conscious helps you to find and know your own mind, something many people have lost connection with in the hurly-burly of modern life.

Repetition is the mother of skill. If you have developed the skill of being confused about your direction, not knowing what you want and failing to get it, then it's time to change your practice.

Decide – Act – Get

Start again and start small. What you're doing here is training your decision-making muscles. Repeated practice making small decisions develops the skill of making bigger decisions. You'll also become hyper conscious of the decisions you are making and you might find, to your surprise, that you've been a bit of a passenger in lots of small areas of your life; simply carried along following the agenda set by others.

If you successfully set out to vacuum your car on Thursday and hit that mark when Thursday comes round then you have all the skills to get what you want. But you must practise, particularly if you have a lifetime of missed goals behind you.

Learning to start small teaches you how to become a Driver **(Part 2)**.

Remember:

If you don't know what you want you will end up working for people who do know what they want. If you don't have an agenda then you will end up working on someone else's agenda.

Key Points: Starting Small

- Start with the smallest possible achievements where you know clearly what you want.

- Make your wanting deliberate. You know what you want, you act, you get it.

- If you fail, go back and pick something even smaller. Teach yourself that you can know what you want and take action to get it.

- Let the big stuff go. Concentrate on building up muscle memory using small achievements.

- Be ready for frequent changes of mind, hesitation and some confusion as you practice listening to what you want.

- Start having an outcome for everything you do. Before each phone call, each meeting, each trip ask yourself, *What do I want from this [meeting]?* and write it down.

Step 2: Start Navigating By Desire

In which we learn the difference between navigating by mood and navigating by desire.

So far...

Starting small and continuing to focus on small wins can change your life but how do you apply this approach to bigger things?

If I Only Did What I Wanted, My Life Would Fall Apart

A question I often get at this point goes something like this:

If I did what I wanted all the time I'd never work or get anything done or achieve anything that needed some effort. And what about all those boring but necessary things that I don't really want to do but have to do, like emptying the washing machine or doing my budget report, which I hate? If I carried on just doing what I wanted, I'm worried that I'd stay in bed all day.

It's a good question, one that comes up a lot, and it brings us to the difference between navigating by mood or navigating by desire.

Your Moods And Your Desires

When we navigate by our moods we are primarily concerned with how we feel so we ask internal questions like, *What do I feel like doing?* or when faced with a choice, *Which one feels right?* or when facing some regular chore we might avoid it if we do not feel like doing it. Can you see a problem with this approach?

I don't know about you but my moods change so much, even what I've just eaten changes how I feel. That makes me a bit wary of using them as a guide and that's why you might be worried about how your life could possibly work if you just did what you felt like all the time.

It could be said that the opposite to mood is desire. Desire is about things that you want rather than things you feel like doing. A lot of the time your mood and your desire are aligned. You feel like a coffee and you want a coffee so you act to get one. With experiences like this it's easy to confuse mood and desire. But what if there is a real difference? You feel like a coffee but you want a good night's sleep. Now you have a clear choice – follow your moods and risk losing sleep, or choose what you really desire instead. Here's a more personal example:

Choosing Desire On A Cold, Wet Morning

Imagine for a moment. It's Saturday morning. 6am. Cold, dark, wet outside and my alarm rings. I surface with a groan in my warm, snuggly bed and realise that, yet again, it's time to get up for my daughter's 6.30am swimming practice. I really do not feel like getting up, I feel like staying in bed. My mood says *don't do it, it's not right for you, it doesn't feel right.*

So I'm lying there and I ask myself, *What do you want?* and I know that even though I do not feel like it, I really do want to get up. In fact I like the quiet time while she is swimming – it's like a little oasis in my week and I've enjoyed it before and I picture myself enjoying it again. I also want to get up because she loves swimming and I want to support her. I still don't feel like it, although, as I begin to think about what I want, my mood is actually changing, coming round to supporting my desire. Eventually I get up.

Learn To Follow Your True Desire

If you can identify your true desire, your mood will fall into line behind it or in plain English: *If there is something you don't feel like doing then maybe you're asking the wrong question.*

Our feelings change so much, affected by the weather, what we eat, the amount of sleep we've had, what we read or watch, the fun or argument we are having. All these affect our mood from moment to moment.

This makes your feelings an unreliable guide to what to do next. Your desires, on the other hand, tend to be deeper and less susceptible to moment by moment changes.

Any time you find yourself in conflict about a simple choice – perhaps you think you should be doing something but don't feel up to it then have a think about what questions you are asking yourself.

If you are navigating primarily by mood you'll be asking, *What do I feel like doing?*

If you are navigating by desire you'll be asking, *What do I really want?*

Anxiety is a sign that you are not focusing on what you want.

As you choose to follow your desires rather than your moods, a couple of things will happen...

Your desires and what you want will become much clearer to you.

Your moods will fall into line behind your desires so that your feelings quickly come to support what you want. And when you feel like doing what you want, it becomes much much easier to start getting what you want.

This Week, Choose Desire

Before you read on, put this book down and take the next week or so to practice navigating by desire. The question is not *What do I feel like* but *What do I want?* Focus on that regardless of whether you feel like doing it or not and notice what happens to your mood. You should find that your feelings eventually start supporting your desires. And remember to keep it small for now so you give those decision making muscles a good workout.

And this brings us right back to the question we started with: *If I only did what I wanted, nothing in my life would get done.*

That's not true though is it? Even if you don't feel like emptying the washing machine, you do want to wear clean clothes. Although you hate doing budget reports you do want to show how well your team has done. In fact, once you stop focusing on how horrible it feels and start thinking about what you desire, you often find that other ideas spring to mind about how to get it done.

63

If you shift your focus away from how you feel towards what you want, it allows you to be more creative. You can worry less about applying this approach to bigger things because even if you don't feel like doing them in the moment, if they are real desires of yours, you can still go with them.

While at first these two ways of making decisions seem similar, they take people in two completely different directions. Since our moods are often tied up in old habits and patterns of thinking, following them tends to just create more of the 'same old, same old' in our lives. Somehow, we just don't get around to making those changes we know we'd love to make, and things that seem like they'll take too much effort are put off until the last minute or don't get done at all.

Your wanting, however, is a living, breathing, fluid process. Each time you do what you want (or don't do what you don't want to do), your actions seem effortless and inspired ideas become almost commonplace. Over time, it becomes easier and easier to read and follow your inner compass. Life gets a lot simpler, and the pursuit of success becomes a lot more fun.

— Michael Neill, www.supercoach.com

Key Points: Desire, Not Mood

- When you navigate by mood you'll find yourself asking, *How do I feel about this?*

- This leaves you open to the vagaries of your changing mind.

- When you navigate by desire you'll find yourself asking, *What do I really want?*

- If you practice following your desire sometimes in spite of your mood then you will begin to recognise your inner compass more easily.

- It's not about how you feel (momentary, fleeting, changeable, happening now) it's about what you want (solid, reassuring, dependable, arrives in the future).

Step 3: Squash The Bugs

As you walk towards the front door you notice those boots that you were going to sell on eBay and sigh to yourself again. The front step is worn and as you leave the house your eye is caught by the peeling paint on the fence rails.

Must call that painter who was working across the road last summer, I've got his number somewhere.

The car door squeaks as you get in and as it starts to rain, the protest from your wipers reminds you that you meant to get a new wiper blade last weekend; only that involves a trip to the other side of town and time ran away with you.

Each one of these is a broken agreement. Promises that you made yourself and have either ignored or not kept. Every single one of them snags a tiny part of your attention, fragmenting it in a thousand different directions. No wonder a clear future is hard to fathom. Why is this?

Your brain has an efficient tracking system for promises you have made yourself and at the same time, almost no awareness of the relative importance of what it is tracking. This means that a casual *note to self* about your new wiper blades has the same priority as your performance review with your boss – at least as far as your brain is concerned.

That Noise Is Bugs, Humming In The Background Of Your Life

What is the effect of this? The first is that these little things bug you constantly. They are a background hum to your life. If you listen carefully you can hear it. Sometimes you can push them all away and other times they spring at you as you wander round the house. You may not realise that you are living with a constant hum of disappointment from all these incomplete items. (If you are unlucky your partner will join in.)

The other main effect is more serious. How would you feel about a friend who constantly let you down? Who promised action and never took it? Who fobbed you off with excuses? Who kept avoiding you when you wanted to talk about what this was doing to your friendship?

You'd fall out wouldn't you?

At the least, communication between the two of you would be strained and it would be difficult to get past these things or talk about more meaningful plans, wouldn't it?

This is how you have been treating yourself. Making easy promises of action and then not doing anything. Discounting or fobbing off any attempt to remind you. Hey, it's no wonder you experience a struggle to draw your attention to the future. Your attention is constantly fragmented in a thousand different directions. What's the answer?

Write Yourself A Bug List, Now!

Do it as soon as you can. Take paper and pen or keyboard and screen and make a list of every incomplete little job that bugs you. (If you have people that bug you, you can put those in a special section of their own.) There may be 50 or more of these. List all the things that annoy you: little jobs, things that need fixing, stuff you've been meaning to do for ages. Imagine someone dropped toast crumbs in the bed of your life. What are all those toast crumbs? List them all.

Now look at the list. Each one has a tiny part of your attention and will continue to occupy this while it remains incomplete. So the next task is to **bring as many of these as possible to completion.** How do you do that?

Rebuild Trust In Yourself

What you have to do is rebuild trust with yourself – exactly as you would have to do if you had been treating a friend this way. You've got to start keeping your agreements or remaking them. And this solution is the same as it would be if you make an agreement with someone else and it becomes obvious you are not going to meet it. You have to:

- Call the person up and remake the agreement.

- Or agree with the person that 'not now' is OK.

- Or agree to end the agreement because you both know it isn't going to happen.

Probably the easiest place to start is with the smallest things in your life. Find the smallest and easiest one on the list and go do it. Keep your promise. As you do this you will notice a tiny release of attention. Pick the next one and go do it.

For each one that you don't do or don't want to do right now, agree with yourself that either:

- You will do it on a certain date.

- Or it no longer needs doing and you are dropping the whole idea.

- Or you are keeping it open but it is not the time to complete it now and you will review it again in seven days time.

Each open loop that you either complete, drop or agree 'not now' will release your attention from that item. You will feel it release, like breathing out and finally realising you were holding your breath the whole time.

Release The Tension And Free Up Your Mind

The point of this is not that you disappear in a mad flurry of action vainly trying to do all the things you have promised yourself. The point is rather to teach you: **To trust yourself.**

And, to be much more careful in the future about what you agree to.

- Each time you make an agreement and either do it or have the courtesy to re-negotiate with yourself, you build confidence that you can trust yourself. That your word counts for something.

- Each time you hold off making a rash promise to yourself you are treating yourself with more maturity and becoming someone who knows the value of their time. And it makes you more of a driver.

- Each time you keep your promise to review the outstanding items, you have reinforced the fact that you can be trusted *and* your brain will let go of tracking these things until the next review.

Be warned though, if you break the promise again, all that will happen is that your brain will pick up the job of tracking them all over again and this means that the moment there is a clear space in your head they will all come to mind, again. That's why they spring at you in the shower, or while you are driving or watching a movie. Your brain thinks *now* is a good time to get some attention on these things: *Hey you, over here, what about all this stuff?* Once you start noticing this happening you will soon start reviewing regularly and stop making rash promises to yourself.

The other point of this is to release your attention so you can turn it to bigger and more meaningful things. It's simply not available at the moment because it is tracking all the unresolved things that bug you.

The good news is that once you close or 'complete for now' loads of these loops you will lose that background tension in your life and gain the space to work on other stuff.

How Does Bug Listing Work?

Figuring out what you want is hard when your attention is diverted by things that bug you and even harder when you cannot trust yourself to keep even the most simple promise. Keep or renegotiate the promises you have already made (get those new wipers, call the painter) and be careful of promises you make from now on. Only say *Yes* if you are going to do it. **Become the kind of person who decides that they need to do something and does it.**

When your attention is free of the little things, I promise you the bigger issues of **direction** and **choice** in your life will begin to emerge like the first snowdrops of spring.

Once you begin to honour the promises you make to yourself or have the maturity to remake the agreement it begins to become much easier to know what you want. As you begin to notice the changes that are happening you'll see yourself edging closer to knowing what you want and being able to get it.

Key Points: Squash The Bugs

- When you notice something that bugs you, you make a mini-promise to yourself. When you do nothing about it, you've broken another promise, more evidence that you cannot trust yourself.

- If something bugs you, however fleeting, it's taking up brain space / energy that distracts you from being clear about what you want.

- Release this energy by using a bug list.

Once a week make a firm decision about every item on the list:

- Handle it, get it done or sorted so that it does not bug you anymore.

- Decide to let it go. Make peace with it.

- Make an agreement with yourself that 'not now' is OK.

- Promise yourself that you will review again next week.

How do you know when something is off the list? Easy. If it starts bugging you again then it isn't taken care of. You can't fool your own brain.

Step 4: Use What You Don't Want

In which we learn how to use what we do not want.

So far...

If you have been acting like a driver and asking yourself what you want on a small level (**Step 1**) you will have discovered something – it does not work all the time and it does not work with everybody.

You may have skipped to this section because asking what you want, even for very small things, simply does not work for you. If you've tried it with others you've probably realised that it doesn't always work for them either.

Here's why and what to do about it:

What Happens When You Ask People What They Want

Let's look first at why it might not work with other people. They may push back if you try too hard to set an agenda before a meeting or quiz them too hard about focusing on their outcomes. And you need to be sensitive to this. But why?

It's Not What You Ask, It's How You Ask

First you have to understand that *What do you want?* is probably the most powerful question in the world – so it can be dangerous in the wrong hands! For people who live like passengers, this question can be disturbing because it implies they are responsible for their results. It calls attention to the difference between what they want and the life they are living now. Sometimes they will react angrily. You have to be sensitive to this.

Tone of voice matters a lot too. Sometimes you need to soften the question a bit, for example:

- *I'm wondering... What is it you really want?*

- *I'm curious... What is it you really want?*

Use a softer tone of voice or you could try asking the question in another way:

- *Just curious, what's your real outcome here?*

- *What's your ultimate outcome?*

Another way is to make it sound like a joint question:

- *What are we really aiming for here?*

- *What are we really hoping to achieve with this?*

- *What's our ultimate outcome?*

Sometimes by gently taking the direct spotlight off someone (*What do we want?*) they will begin to think of a wider range of ways to get that result for themselves.

Why *What Do You Want?* Can Be A Useless Question

These suggestions might be enough to help you if you've been a bit pushy with your new found zeal to think about what you want but there's more to this than meets the eye. Some people really don't like this question and in fact, for about 50% of the population the question *What do you want?* is totally useless.

You see, unless you are a highly motivated, goal-seeking person who relentlessly uses positive language all the time, the chances are that you spend at least some of your time thinking about things you don't like and don't want.

Remember the boy on the wall? Some of us have had years of practice focused on the downside, the dangers, what could go wrong and what we don't want to happen. We've been working hard to reinforce this and if we are parents, we can probably hear ourselves doing it to our children as well. We're good at it.

And this is why *What do you want?* may not have worked for some people. Because it is such a foreign and sometimes intrusive question. Even now, I sometimes seize up and go completely blank when I ask myself that question. We've had no practice with it and for some people, it is such a contrast to their normal thinking that it just does not work.

Why Motivational Speeches Rarely Work

For most people, listening to this kind of motivational talk only serves to reinforce the barely acknowledged belief that *It's all right for them, but I'm just not like that.*

Thankfully, help is at hand. All you have to do is learn to use what you **don't** want. And since at least half the population are good at this, you should find it easy to use with yourself and with them.

Are You A Towards Or Away From Person?

Remember my car example? Having a firm focus on the downside, on the danger, on what you do not want is a bit like driving around by only looking in the rear view mirror. You reverse away from what you don't like until you sort of find somewhere where there is nothing so bad that you need to move away from it.

We call this an **Away From** motivation because it describes someone who moves away from pain rather than towards pleasure. It's the classic pattern of the yo-yo dieter. When I reach 210 pounds I hate it, feel fat and uncomfortable, clothes no longer fit well so I'm highly motivated to move away from this. It's too painful. As I successfully lose weight, though, the pain lessens and as the pain fades away, so does my motivation. As my motivation fades, back comes the weight. So I yo-yo.

Yes, it is nuts. I gain weight as a way of gaining motivation. It's the classic pattern of the person who waits for things to get bad before doing something about it. How many people do you know who stay in a job, or relationship or social life that they don't like but is not bad enough to do anything about? How many people do you know who talk about *No pain, no gain* or describe gritting their teeth and making themselves do things. These are the **Away From** people.

And, for them, goals just do not work because they lack the essential motivation of having to move away from something.

The Second Most Powerful Question In The World

I promised you the second most powerful question in the world and here it is. If you are an **Away From** person or you know people who are primarily motivated this way then asking them *What do you want?* probably does not work. Much better is the question *What do you want, [pause] instead?*

Think of something trivial within a few feet of where you are sitting, something you do not like. For example, let's say the menu system on your phone is confusing and you're always forgetting how to find the settings.

Now watch what happens when I ask you *What do you want, [pause] instead?*

Perhaps what you want instead is a menu system that is easy to use, where the choices are obvious. Something that looks as if it has been designed for normal people. See how quickly your focus has changed, instead of moaning about the phone you're now thinking about the solution.

First you go with your natural focus – the moan, the irritation or the thing you don't like. Then ask yourself *What do I want, [pause] instead?*

To answer you have to take your eyes off the rear view mirror and glance in some other direction. The question causes you to search around until you find something you like; then you can steer towards it.

It also feels different because it releases different chemicals in the body. And it changes the script you run in your head. You may not have been aware how negative that script was until you try this.

And the best thing of all is that it is totally non-threatening. *What do you want instead?* You'll find you need to be gentle with the **Away From** people, and yourself, because you and they are out of practice. You may have to ask this several times and catch them if it turns into a complaint again.

Give Your Children Something To Move Towards

If you are an **Away From** parent, your communication style may well be full of warnings and lurid descriptions of the consequences of things going wrong – *don't run across the road, you'll be killed!*

You owe it to your children to give them the option of considering what they should move towards as well. Just because you use consequences and pain to motivate yourself does not mean this works for your children.

So just as you are about to yell *don't run across the road, you'll be killed* consider what thought you want to leave them with instead: *remember to look both ways and use the crossing, wait until the traffic stops and get across safely.* Their preferred motivator may be moving towards something. If nothing else, remembering to do both makes you a more fully rounded communicator.

Practice rolling the words around your tongue: *What do you want, instead?*

Let me give you a couple more examples of this in action.

What Do You Want, Instead?

Once, a long time ago, I was doing regular reviews with my team leaders when I saw this question work like a dream. Let's call her Chris. She was a new team leader and this was her first review with me. I started in the normal way: *How's it going?* This unleashed a stream of complaints, moans, things she didn't like, things she thought we were doing badly etc.

I waited for her to finish and then said: *OK Chris, thanks for that, it's quite a list, so what do you want instead?* There was a long silence while she processed the question and then admitted that she didn't know.

Why don't you go and have a think about what you want instead? Come back and we'll make a plan to make some changes.

Off she went. She had come to the meeting with her focus so firmly fixed on what she did not want (and did not like and wanted to move away from) that she had barely thought about what she wanted to move towards. She had arrived with problems without bringing any solutions.

This question *What do you want instead?* will help you and the people you work with understand what they want to move **towards**.

Moans, complaints, whines, disillusionment, anger, disappointment, blame, dissatisfaction are all symptoms of a passenger mentality. Being asked *What do you want instead?* naturally helps them search around for something they want to move towards and helps them become more of a driver.

Practise this. Ask yourself and ask others. When your children complain about something ask them *What do you want instead?* When your colleagues complain about the rubbish TV they watched at the weekend ask them *What would prefer to watch instead?* When tempted to complain about your boss ask yourself *What do I want instead?* When you hear yourself keeping up a running commentary of dissatisfaction tell yourself *OK, I hear you. Now, what do you want instead?*

Remember, anxiety (and moaning) are a sign that you are not focusing on what you want.

Here's another story where I nearly made a huge mistake by not paying attention to different motivational styles.

Joanne And The Budget

I learned about the effect of **towards** and **away from** communication the hard way, by managing people. I am a natural **Away From** person. I routinely leave things until they get so bad I have to change them (until the pain gets bad enough). My default way of motivating myself is to remind myself of the consequences of 'not doing' and issue warnings to myself about what to watch out for. Because this is the default way of motivating myself I tend to use it (if I'm not careful) as my default style when communicating with others.

I remember calling a meeting with my team leaders about the state of our budget. We had done well against a stiff debt collection target but we needed to do better.

Jo was sitting opposite me and, as I launched into a series of warnings, admonitions and what if's, I could see her motivation literally draining away.

To my horror, I could see that the more I talked the more I managed to turn off her motivation. You see, I knew something about Jo. She was my star debt collector, motivated, committed and relentless and here I was doing my best to drain it all away. What I knew about Jo was that she was the kind of person who was virtually 100% **towards** in everything she did. What motivated her were targets, achievement, restless energy towards a goal and hitting milestones. In other words I was using the wrong strategy, I was communicating with my star player using my preferred style not hers; I was communicating with my star player in exactly the opposite way to how she best motivated herself.

Fortunately when I saw this happening I was able to adjust, but it was a close call. I could have walked from that meeting leaving my team leaders limp and drained of motivation. Has this ever happened to you?

If you find yourself focused firmly on the downside, collecting uncomfortable situations as a way of charging up your motivation then it's time to play with *What do you want instead?* Whenever you communicate with others make sure you give the **Away From** people things to avoid and the **Towards** people things to aim at.

Learn To Use What You Don't Want

This is great but how do you use this to help know what you want?

All of us have a bit of **Away From** focus in our lives and for this next week I want you to unearth as many as you can dig up. I want you to find all the questions or parts of your life where you spend more time thinking about what you don't want or don't like instead of what you want.

Here's the exercise. Start with something simple again like, say, your job. Now think of something you don't like about your job. For example: *I don't like breathing recycled air all day.* Write that down on the left.

Then ask yourself the question *What do I want instead?* and write down whichever answer or answers come to mind. It could be anything from *I want an outdoor job* to *I want to go for a walk at lunchtime.*

Start simple and start with a good moan about all the things you do not like or do not want. Also include those things that you know you don't want in the future – capture them all – even things like *I never want to be an accountant.* Aim for quantity here rather than quality. Then follow the instructions on the sheet.

It might be a big list.

Exercise: Use What You Don't Want

If you are good at knowing what you **don't** want then take advantage of this. Use it to reveal to yourself what you actually want instead.

How To Use The Exercise

Pick a life area like, say, **My Job** then on the left hand side make a list of all the things that you don't want, don't like, annoy you, or you dislike. Do your best to make them specific:

- I don't like that I can't see the sun where I sit
- I hate being interrupted all the time
- I'm fed up with the travelling
- I never want to be an accountant

And so on:

Empty your complaints onto the page, capture everything, big and small. Have a good moan on paper and dwell on this for a bit.

*Given a choice, if I had a totally free hand, **what don't I want to have** in my job?*

Got it all? OK now take the first one and ask yourself **What do I want, instead?** Give this a little bit of thought, it may be the opposite or it may be something quite different. Note down your answers.

- *I don't like that I can't see the sun where I sit.*
- ***What do I want instead?***
- *Actually what I want is to be outside more often, (funny, I never realised that before).*
- ***I want to work with nature not numbers.***

Take each dislike or don't want in turn and note down your answer to the question *What Do I Want Instead?*

Life Area: eg My Job		
I don't want...		I do want...
START HERE Make a list of all the things you don't want in your job.	**What do you want instead?**	FINISH HERE Fill this side up with what you want instead.

Your List of Wants

When you've done this, look at what you've got. You've clearly identified all the things you don't want in your job or a job. You've asked yourself what you want instead and you now have at least some idea of this written down. This gives you things to move away from and things to move towards.

As we've already said, just moving away from what you don't like is like driving while only looking in the rear view mirror. It's bumpy and slow. Now you are beginning to look forward as well. Not only do you know what to move away from but you know a bit more clearly which direction to go in. This will stop you finding yourself in yet another random place that you have to move away from.

Setting some sort of forward direction is much quicker than reversing out of one place after another.

Now pick a different area of your life and repeat the exercise. Pick a harder one, perhaps where things are a bit fuzzy.

Have Fun Using This New Skill

This question *What do you want instead?* is a new life skill for you. Have fun using it. Whenever you catch yourself moaning or complaining or muttering about something ask yourself *OK, what do I want instead?*

Notice what this does.

You hear a different conversation in your head, it feels lighter and you can see a new direction more clearly as you lift your head up from whatever is annoying you.

Play with using it with partners, children, and friends. It works with colleagues and superbly well with bosses. Have a go. The only thing you have to watch is your voice tone and way of asking it. You may need to soften it a bit:

- *So, I'm curious, what do you want instead?*

- *So what do you want to watch on TV?* (when they moan about TV?)

- *So, what is your ideal job then?* (when griping about work)

- *So, what should we do instead?* (when your boss complains)

What you are doing here is helping people become drivers because the only way they can answer the question *What do you want instead?* is to get up from their passenger seat and walk to the front of the bus. It's a form of social service to the world. Have fun with it.

Download The Workbook

At *www.firstknowwhatyouwant.com* you can find your **'First Know Journal'** to print and use with these exercises. Print it as many times as you like and share with friends.

Quick Read: Use What You Don't Want

We've known this for a long, long, time and it still amazes me how little attention we pay to this basic aspect of how the brain works.

If I say to you, *Don't think of a blue frog,* what hops into your mind? Something blue and froggy has appeared inside your head despite a specific instruction not to.

It seems that **our brains can only process information positively** so a command like *Don't think of a blue frog* gets processed like this *Do – think of blue frog – Not.* Do think about something positively and then negate it. That's why a blue frog appears when I tell you not to think of one.

Use Your Brain Chemistry To Know What You Want

If you know that this is how negative commands get processed you can see how you may actually be getting your mind to dwell on things that you didn't intend. *Don't think of a blue frog* leaves a blue frog in your mind. *I don't want to get fat and out of condition* leaves an image of you fat and out of condition in your mind. *Don't rush this you'll spoil it* leaves you with a clear image of rush and spoil.

This is confusing. Especially as your brain chemistry tries to assist you in getting more of what you dwell on. If you keep inadvertently giving it examples of negative results to dwell on, is it any wonder that those things tend to show up more?

Don't hesitate to call us means *Do – hesitate to call us – not* which has quite a different impact from the one the writer intended!

The solution is to learn to give yourself (and others) only positive suggestions. If I want you to avoid those blue frogs then instead of saying *Don't think of a blue frog* I need to say *Think about green frogs* and voilà, green frogs appear in your head.

How To Put Images In Someone's Head

This is equally true when talking to other people because the things you say and the way you say them actually put images inside other peoples heads. You do it all the time. *Let's think about green frogs for a minute* and the green frogs duly appear inside them. It's powerful, especially if you have any kind of teaching role, management responsibilities or children. Keep your language positive. Talk only about what you want them to dwell on.

A warning though. Using positive language can be quite hard to do (note your reaction) if you have always been brought up to focus on what could go wrong or the downside of any situation. I find that the first draft of anything I write or produce is overwhelmingly focused on what to move away from, full of negative commands and warnings.

This used to worry me but now I accept it as the result of years of conditioning. I accept that my first draft will always be like this. I deliberately go over my first draft and change the writing to balance all the **Away From** stuff with more positive statements.

Towards Or Away From

How did you get up this morning? Some people are **Towards** people. What motivates them is moving towards what they want. They wake up and run through all the things they want to do today. This gets them out of bed eager to get on with their day. Some people though are **Away From** people. What motivates them is moving away from what they don't want or don't like. They move away from pain. They will stay in bed until the pain and possible consequences of staying in bed are worse than the pain of getting up. Then they will move.

If you are a natural **Away From** person (as I am) you will be used to using pain as a motivator. Your language is of the *don't think of a blue frog* variety. You tend to stay with situations until the pain gets so bad that you have to move. If this is you, you have some work to do. Begin to notice how you speak to yourself. Pay attention to what you say yourself. Begin to practice using positive language so that you leave your mind dwelling on the things you want.

What Do You Want, Instead?

If you are a natural **Away From** person and particularly as you begin to notice this in others you'll also find that it's not quite as simple as using positive language. In fact being relentlessly positive will be a turn off for about half the people you meet – not quite what you intended.

For these folks you have to be more subtle. Remember the power of language to rewire another persons thoughts?

Use the question *What do you want instead?* Or *What's a better alternative?* or *If you could not have that result any more, what would you want in its place?* or any variation of this question.

When you ask they have to set aside their focus and search around for a more positive alternative. Even if they don't immediately know the answer just attempting to answer it means a person has to get out of their passenger seat walk to the front of their bus and sit down in the drivers seat.

If you are a natural **Towards** person I'm surprised you have read this far. If you have, then I suggest you start having fun with seeing what you can get other people to think about. Remember that almost anything you say creates an image in their heads. Imagine how useful this could be in a meeting, a presentation or a sales situation. Play with it.

How To Defeat The Office Whiner

You know them. The friend who deflates you with their complaining. The colleague who keeps up a litany of dissatisfaction. Your relative who only rings to whine about life. You want to be polite but frankly they get you down and you're sick of providing free listening therapy. Next time, use this question: *What do you want instead?*

Every time you hear a *don't want, don't like, not happy with* ask them (gently, lovingly) *What do you want instead?*

Keep doing it. Either the quality of the conversation will improve and they will thank you for being such a great listener or they will begin to avoid you. Either way it's a win.

How To Unstick A Team With Reverse Brainstorming

Here's a way of using the *don't want* focus to unstick a sticky situation. Got a team that are stuck in their ways, or complacent, or bored with your meetings? Got a child stuck with their school work? Got a spouse who's beginning to complain about their life? Use their *don't want* focus to unstick them by doing a reverse brainstorm:

- *How can we make this situation worse?*

- *How can we make sure you get totally lousy grades? Let's make a plan.*

- *How can we make sure you turn into a proper grumpy old man, what else do you need to do?*

Reverse brainstorming, or deliberately looking for ways to make a situation worse than it is, makes people laugh. It takes them by surprise and changes their focus by sneaky use of brain neurology. I livened up some interview training once by getting the group to generate ideas for ensuring that their interviews were an objectionable failure. Try it. It works because in order to think about how to make things worse you have to consider what would make them better.

Stuck? Do a reverse brainstorm with yourself: *What do I need to do so I make this situation even worse?*

It's impossible to do this without thinking of how to make it better.

What could we both do to make this marriage worse? might lead to a lot of sheepish laughter and a break in the deadlock.

85

Key Points: Use What You Don't Want?

- Be clear about what you don't want. Then ask yourself *What do I want instead?*

- If you find yourself navigating by moving away from what you don't like, ask yourself *What would I like to move towards instead?*

- If all else fails, think about how you could make your situation much, much worse.

- Remember you mind looks for the positive value in everything so it will look for the positive value in what you are thinking about. If you are thinking about how fat you are, your mind will focus on delivering fat to you because that is clearly what you are looking for.

- If you had a built-in result-seeking missile that would operate 24 hours a day without your conscious involvement, what would you give it to do? Guess what...

- When you are negative or feeling low, this is hard to do but the way out is not dwelling on what is wrong or not working. It's by asking *What do I want instead?*

Step 5: Make A Wish List

In which we learn how to make all your wishes come true.

So far...

Annoying isn't it? If you have been using the question *What do you want instead?* **(Step 4)** then you've probably lost something.

When I first started using it, I discovered that I couldn't moan any more. I used to enjoy a good whinge and whine to myself but now what happens is I have a little voice that pops up in my head and asks me *What do you want instead?* and that ruins my bad mood. I use it with my teenagers and it's hard not to laugh when it ruins their bad mood as well – it's powerful and easy to use.

If you've noticed this happening too, then take it as a sign that you are becoming a driver **(Part 2)**. Many people who live like a passenger use their moods as a way of excusing themselves from taking action and one of the downsides of learning to be a driver is letting go of a lot of this. I'm not guaranteeing no more bad moods but I can guarantee a way out if you want to take it.

Let's move on. So far we have looked at small wins, using small achievements to practice deciding what you want, taking action and noticing that you've got it **(Step 1)**. Then we looked at reversing your whole approach and putting your focus firmly on what you don't want as a way of using your existing **Away From** skills **(Step 4)**.

Now we're going to look at your daydreams for clues about what you want for your life.

If I could show you a way to make your dreams come true would you be interested?

Are You Nurturing A Fantasy?

Almost anything you want is within your grasp if you are willing to make a plan and work the plan.

Let me tell you about one of my dreams...

For years I had this fantasy of learning to ride a motor-bike. Me, on a Harley, with a ponytail, bandana, shades and a leather jacket with tassels. All I actually managed to get was the Harley belly. But I loved to talk about it, especially with friends who did ride bikes. This went on for ages until one day, one of them asked me, *Why don't you just go and do it?* And then it struck me, I didn't have a good reason not to.

What do you wish for? If I had a magic wand and could grant you unlimited wishes then what? You can have anything you like in your daydreams. What takes your fancy? Anything. What dreams, wishes or regular fantasies do you have? Even the things that you know are beyond your grasp. I'll give you a minute to think about it.

So, those things you just been thinking about, how long have you been carrying these around in your head without doing anything about it? A long time? Years, some of them?

Is there anything you talk about, even to yourself, but have never done anything about? You see, I'd never done anything about my bike fantasy because it seemed over-whelming. The time for the lessons, buying a bike – how was I going to afford that? Then the business of passing a test. We'd just had a baby and I had my hands full. In fact I had a lot of handy excuses.

Nothing happened until I gave serious attention to what I would actually have to *do*. Once I worked out the main steps and put them in some kind of order I began to see that I could break it down into fairly small actions and take them one at a time.

Eating Your Elephants

Most wishes remain as wishes because they never get connected to any real steps and then never developed into easy, straightforward actions. It's like that old proverb: *How do you eat an elephant?*

If you were given the task of eating an elephant, how would you do it? The main thing you know is that you can only do it one mouthful at a time. And before you could get to mouthfuls you'd have to kill it, then saw it into large chunks and divide those chunks into smaller chunks until you had a mouth sized portion. Only then could you begin to eat. Given enough time you could eat the whole thing – one mouthful at a time.

What are your elephants? Your big, unobtainable wishes that are going nowhere?

Why not stop a moment and make a list, before we go any further? Here are some examples:

- *I've always wanted a boat, one that the family could use. I'd like to teach my children about boats.*

- *I like music and always fancied learning the piano or something else.*

- *And New Zealand, there's a country I'd like to tour, but I cannot see us ever having time for that.*

Got your list? Good. Now this week what I want you to do is have a serious go at connecting these wishes to the steps needed to make them come true.

First you need to sketch out the big steps you'd need to take to turn that wish into reality. Next you need to take each step and break it down into tiny, single step actions (mouthfuls).

What's a single step action?

A single step action is something like *open drawer, turn on television, print document*. In other words its a small enough action that if I wrote it on a card and gave it to someone they could go and do it.

So far, so good but why think about wishes that don't stand a chance of coming true?

Grab a pen and draw yourself a cloud shape at the top of the page. Print the word **FANTASY** inside it. These wishes, (eg your desire to own a boat) are fantasies. They float around in your head and you take them out every so often to polish them. Then you consign them to the back of your mind with a wistful look while you get back to reality.

Now draw a circle somewhere else on your page and print the word **STEPS** inside it. Join it to the cloud with a line. Next draw an arrow down from **STEPS** and print **ACTIONS** at the bottom of your paper.

This process is your chance to challenge what you are doing by linking these fantasies to the major steps that would make them real and then breaking down those steps in to a number of easy action steps. When you do this I'm willing to bet that two things will happen.

- You will get excited because a fantasy suddenly looks to be within your grasp.

- Or once you appreciate the commitment required to make it happen you will decide that it is not for you.

Either way, it will no longer be a fantasy taking up space in your head. Dealing with it either by dismissing it for good or making a real plan will free up space to focus on other things that you want.

Let's look at a real example. One that always comes up in a workshop when I am challenged about this.

How To Win The Lottery

Most wishes remain as wishes because they never get connected to any steps and the steps never get connected to any actions. And without having bite-sized actions to do, you are never going to do anything are you? To discover the reality of what you want you'll have to bring your wishes down to the action level and then you will know whether your wish is a deep hidden desire that will fulfil you if you get it or just one of those cosy fantasies that you take out and play with every so often.

So, go ahead and pick something that you wish for. Pick anything. Even silly things that you think you have no chance of making real. In fact, this works better with outrageous wishes.

Example: **I wish that I would win the lottery.**

(If this process is as good as I claim then it should be able to get you a lottery win. Agreed?)

Let's leave aside for a moment that this is probably covering up a true wish for other things like, say, more freedom and control, and go with the lottery thing.

First, let's chop the problem into large chunks or big steps. What steps could you take to ensure a lottery win? No analysis, just an unrestrained brain dump. Pick up your pen and fire away…

Chop Your Fantasy Into Chunks

You could…

- Buy every single ticket for this draw.

- Break into the TV studio and tamper with the balls.

- Build a replica machine and smuggle it into the studio.

- Bribe a cameraman to cut to a piece of stock footage so I am the only one to see the true draw.

- Marry a millionaire who could afford to buy me all the draw tickets

Stop there a moment. Too silly? It might seem silly but do you agree that all of these are possible steps to a lottery win?

If so, and with more time, you'd need to keep going until you had every step that it is possible to take in pursuit of a lottery win (remember, with no judgement or worry about realism or legality).

Chop Each Chunk Into Mouthfuls

For now though let's use one example and break it down into single-step actions, small enough to go on a card.

Let's assume for a moment that you were going to build a replica machine and smuggle it into the studio. What would you have to do first?

What about getting hold of the plans for an existing one?

And to do that?

Perhaps you could bribe an employee where they make them.

But you don't know where they are made, do you? So what is the smallest step before that?

I suppose..., what about..., I know, it's to navigate to the Google home page to start a search.

So now we have an action, a single step action small enough to go on a card. Grab a stack of index cards and get busy writing one action per card.

Elephant To Chunk To Mouthful, or Fantasy to Steps To Actions

Do you see what we've done here?

We have taken a vague wish, brainstormed the steps and then broken down one step to the point where we have a tiny action to take, in this example, open a browser and find the Google home page.

What you need to do now is take each step and break it down into bite-sized actions until you can answer the question *What's the next action?* Then you'll have a 1,000-step action plan to win the lottery and if you do every step you could win it. Suddenly, it is no longer a fantasy. You have a plan.

Hang on a minute.

Whoa! At this point you might be thinking, *That's loads of work, I don't want to do all of that and I'm not sure that half of it would work anyway.* (And some of it is illegal).

Once you hit this point you've answered your own question haven't you? You've discovered that although, like many people, you have a lottery fantasy; when confronted with all the work required to make it happen you've lost your appetite for it. What you need to do now is pick another fantasy to work with or ask yourself what your desire for a lottery win was covering up.

Use the exercise on the next page. Pick another fantasy, perhaps that boat idea or the New Zealand tour and do it again.

Exercise: Make A Wish List

Turn your wishes into actions. Someone once told me that you could have anything you want if you were willing to ask 1,000 people. Or achieve any goal if only you were willing to think of 1,000 actions and then do them.

How To Use The Exercise

Make a list of all your wishes. All of them. Even the ones you don't think you have a chance of getting.

Pick one.

Do a wild, unhinged brainstorm of all the likely or possible steps you could take to make this happen.

Pick one.

Break it down into one or many bite size actions that are small enough to start today.

I wish...	How could I? (Steps or Options)	What would I need to do? (Actions)

When you have finished, you should have:

- 1 x wish
- 50 x steps (or more)
- 1,000 x actions (or more)

Link your wish to the major steps you could take, then link each step to the actions required to achieve it. Make each action small enough that it is a single item. If you want to, write each action on an index card and carry the stack around with you.

Now you have a plan. If you want this wish to come true you just need to do the 1,000 or so small actions and it's yours.

Decide whether you want this or not.

- If you do, take one or more of the actions – what are you waiting for?

- If you don't, pick another one of your wishes and start the process again.

Download The Workbook

At *www.firstknowwhatyouwant.com* you can find your **'First Know Journal'** to print and use with these exercises. Print it as many times as you like and share with friends.

Quick Read: Make A Wish List

Making a wish list works like a cash-flow forecast for a new business. It helps you to confront the reality of the actions needed to make something happen. Many people end their lives with *What if?* or *If only* fantasies that never got beyond a daydream.

Chop your daydreams into rough chunks. Chop the chunks into mouthfuls and you can eat an elephant. Connect your daydreams with real steps and then those steps with real actions, giving you a route map to make any wish come true.

Having done the process and realised that with enough small actions you can make anything happen, you may realise that you don't want it or are not prepared to put in the work to make it happen.

That's OK. The important thing is that you come to some agreement with yourself about what you are going to do with this.

Is It A True Wish or Fantasy Comfort Blanket?

If it is a true wish of yours then you can make it happen *if* you are willing to work out the steps and take the actions. Anything is possible with this method. What might happen though is that you look at the actions and realise you do not want to do any of them. Or you get overwhelmed by the process and give up. Either way you have learned something.

You've either learned that what you wish for is possible and you have an outline plan. Or you've learned that you don't want it at all or not enough to do anything about it. Your wishes might just be a comfort blanket that you take out to suck thoughtfully from time to time.

You could:

- Keep it as a fantasy and daydream about it every so often just to enjoy the dream.
- Dismiss it forever.

- Keep it on a *might do, one day* list and agree to review this list every six months or so.

- Start taking action.

- Redefine it as a smaller goal that gives you the part of it you do want.

- Ask yourself what achieving that would give you (more freedom?) and look for another way to get the same result.

Whatever you do after working through this exercise, you can free yourself from the torture of having wishes that you tell yourself you either can't or won't have.

Once you realise that anything is possible you may start to think of other things you want.

It can be daunting to realise that almost anything you want is within your grasp – *if* you are willing to make a plan and work the plan.

You Have No Idea What You Are Capable Of

I used to coach clients to set realistic goals. Until I opened a magazine and read about a man who was still running marathons after losing the lower half of both legs. I realised then that we are just not capable of setting realistic goals. Why? Because our awareness of what is realistic for us is so stunted that we simply have no real idea of what we are capable of.

History shows that with enough time and enough flexibility a human being can achieve almost anything they set their heart on. It's almost certain that whatever you think is realistic for you is a mere fraction of what you are capable of. In fact there is only one real way to find out what you are capable of and that is to start doing it.

The only way to know your limits is to find them – you can't do it by imagining what they are.

Key Points: Using Your Wish List

- Somebody once told me *You can have anything you want if you are willing to ask 1,000 people.*

- Where do you bale out? After three people, five, 10?

- To make any dream come true start by breaking it down into big chunks.

- Then break each chunk down into tiny action steps, small enough to put on an index card and give to a stranger to do.

- Don't fancy this? Too much work? Then your dream is probably a fantasy – keep it around if you like but don't torture yourself about it. Find another dream that you are prepared to work on.

Step 6: Find Your Talents

Have you ever felt that if only you had an obvious talent it would be easy to work out what you wanted?

Once upon a time, a king was about to set out on a long journey. He called all his servants together and assigned them some money to invest while he was away. To one he gave 10 talents of silver, to another five and some servants only got one.

Look after these talents, he told them; *put them to good use because I'll want to see how my investment has done when I come back.*

You probably know the end of the story but something has always bothered me about it. What if you do not know what your talents are? What if you are a reasonably bright person, living in a modern country, who could do almost anything? You are probably good at loads of things but none of them stand out as something you would call a talent.

This is a common problem among people who do not know what they want. When you look at others with an obvious talent it seems unfair that their decision is so easy, they don't struggle to define their path in life. After all they are a great piano player so it's pretty obvious what they should spend their time doing, isn't it?

Frankly, you are going nowhere with this approach. Comparing your life to the hyper-talented will just make you unhappy, particularly if you compare yourself to the most ridiculous example you can find. You look at Leonardo Da Vinci's sketchbooks and then glance back at yours. Instant depression! (And a complete lack of motivation).

So how do you solve this talent conundrum? How do you discover your talents in a way that might help you pick a direction or some momentum for your life. Here's how:

- First you need to know how to find them. What they look like and how to know what yours are.

- Next you need to understand that talents vary with context. What is a talent in one situation is useless in others.

- And lastly understand that talents a) need coaxing and b) appear at different times in your life.

Find Your Talents

There they are, sitting right under your nose. A talent is something you do so easily and so naturally that you probably don't even notice it. But you can learn to.

I love making presentations. I love working with Keynote to make slides, for me it is easy and fluid. When I sit at the keyboard with a few ideas, good, visual slides just fly off the end of my fingers. And here's the thing. I cannot understand why some other people find it so hard. I have sat with people who have laboured so slowly over it that it makes me wince. Once – and I'm not proud of this – I shouldered someone out of the way and did it for them because I couldn't bear the pain of watching them stumble through it.

This happened a lot at one stage of my career. I just could not understand why if it was so easy for me, it wasn't easy for them. It took ages for me to admit to myself that I might have a talent for making slides.

Do you have examples like this? Do you have skills or abilities (even minor ones) where you cannot understand why other people make such a deal out of something so easy? Do you wince when you watch someone else do it badly?

Congratulations, you have just identified a talent.

Your Talents Appear To Be Nothing Special

When you face up to your talents they will surprise you because, to you, they are nothing special. Your talents are the things you do, like breathing, that don't take a special effort. That's the point and that's what makes it a talent. To you it's like breathing while to the rest of us it looks like a gift.

What do you enjoy so much it does not feel like work? What kinds of things do you do, just for the pleasure of doing them? These might be talents too.

Talents Vary With Context

Let's go back to my talent with presentations. It's not a fixed thing is it? It's not always a talent. I have worked in teams where at least four of us can do the same thing, some even better than me. In that context it's a useful backup skill but not a talent.

I have also worked in teams where this talent shone because I was the best available at the time.

Your talents vary with context. Sometimes you sparkle and sometimes there is no room for your talent to shine.

It's less a question of *what are your talents?* and more a question of *am I in the right place to allow my talents to shine?* Maybe a change of time or place would allow you to see your talent more clearly.

Stories abound of these kinds of revelations. The office supply clerk who chances across a tango class and realises she has a talent for teaching. The civil servant who invents a fantasy world to liven up his job and discovers people will pay him to write about it.

Coaxing Your Talents

Do you know the end of the story we started with? The king comes back and asks for an investment update. Most of the servants had put their talents to work and increased the original value. One poor soul refused to take a risk with his talent and just buried it. The king is less than pleased with this approach.

Stumbling across a talent of yours is only the beginning. It will often start with something you can do much more easily than others. Perhaps you find it easy to move to music or you pick up notes quickly or you know how to structure a meeting agenda to get the best out of a group of people. Once you have an inkling of a talent, you'll need to fan it into flame otherwise you'll not get the full benefit and nor will anyone else.

One of the great lies of creativity is that talented people can produce great things with relatively little work. This is just not true. Behind every great musician or singer lie hours and hours of practice. Look closely at the lives of every great writer and you see days and days of revising and rewriting. Sometimes years of toil. It's the same for every great talent you see. What you are looking at is the skill that comes with thousands of hours of practice to hone it to perfection.

The Crucial Difference Between Talent And Skill

These inklings of talent, things you enjoy doing, stuff you notice that comes easier to you than others, are gifts from God, given to you so that you can find a place in the world and find work that satisfies you. What talent does is get you in the door, it gets you started with a shove in the right direction.

Skill is what happens when you develop your talent so that it benefits you and others. Unfortunately skill only comes with hundreds of hours of working at your craft. Repetition is the mother of skill, doing it over and over again as you hone your talents into something magnificent.

Which is why, if you get a sniff of one of your talents you should grab every chance to practise it. It seems to be God's plan that hard work be satisfying, not easy, but accompanied by a profound sense of satisfaction. And so here we have all the clues we need. It's something you enjoy, you can do it more easily than others, you find yourself willing to work hard at it and doing so is satisfying. Put those together and you are in the presence of a talent.

And with a clear view of your talents it's much easier to decide what you want to do next.

Some of your talents you'll be able practise because of what you do for a living. If you have a knack for running meetings then it's pretty easy to volunteer (or be volunteered) to do this more often. And you should until you make it look effortless. For other talents though you'll have to go out of your way to practise them.

When You Love It But Are Not Very Good

This is particularly true of things you love doing but your skill level is low. Often this is a latent talent that needs some work. The love you have for it signals that it is natural and fits you well but the skill level tells you that you need to practice. I love riding my motorbike but it's taken me years to get any level of skill at going fast around corners. A novice rider looking at my cornering now might be impressed. It may even look like a gift. But they cannot see the hours of poor braking, wrong lines and late gear changes that have dogged my cornering. Only because I liked it so much did I persevere.

There's a virtuous circle of finding your talents and it goes like this:

If you enjoy something will you do it more or less? More. And if you do something more do you tend to get better or worse at it? Better. And if you get better at doing something do you tend to enjoy it more or less? See the circle? When you have found your talents and put the hours in to become skilled you have found one of your niches in life and the source of much future pleasure.

Some gifts arrive fully formed and just need polish while others are a bit like flat pack furniture. You get an idea of what's it's like but it's going to take some work to put it together. If your skill level is low then use your love to motivate you to practice repeatedly and bring the talent to life. You'll find it so annoying when others tell you how lucky you are to have this gift but my tip is just to smile graciously and encourage them to find their own talents.

As Your Life Turns, So Do Your Talents

Until I became a father I had no idea I could entertain an audience of small children with dramatic readings and no idea that I could function well on half my normal sleep. Life changed and pulled new talents out of me as it did.

This natural process happens to anyone who stays open to new ideas and new ways of doing things. Retain your youthful willingness to go to different places, seek out new experiences and try new stuff. You have latent talents which you will never know about until circumstances help you discover them. Your future will definitely reveal new talents you didn't know you had.

If thinking about your talents has you completely stumped then it could be that you have not had enough life experiences. Go and do something different. Take a risk or two. Seek new adventures until you shock your system into revealing new loves, wants and talents.

Use the exercise to reflect on some of these.

Remember, Talents, Not Talent

That's the annoying thing about the obviously gifted celebrity or sports person. They have this one thing, one obvious talent that makes all their decision making easy (or so it seems). Most people are not like this, you might not be. Most people have been handed a potful of talents, big and small, to make something with.

Searching for your One Big Thing is misleading and can cause a lot of heartache. This isn't about throwing your job to become a dance instructor because you like dancing. Most likely you'll have an assemblage of talents and plenty of chances to practise many of them. It's about you understanding the patchwork you have and knitting it together to form a life that is pleasurable to live (and keeps you warm).

Know Who You Are To Know What You Want

Seeing your talents in stark relief might help you to know more about what you want. Imagine creating a life where even if you work hard your work is not only deeply satisfying but benefits others as well. Imagine days spent doing the things that fit you well. It's a bit like discovering a brand of clothes that feel like a second skin. Why wear anything else?

Think hard about finding times and places that allow you to express your talent and hone it to a sharp point. We need you.

Exercise: Find Your Talents

Your talents are sitting there in plain sight. They are the things you do so naturally you may have overlooked them. Remember, it's not how you view them that matters, it's how they look to the rest of us.

How To Use The Exercise

Easy For You

Make a list of all the things you find dead easy but you notice that other people struggle with. Make a particular note of things that are as natural as breathing but don't appear to be so for others. My list would start like this:

- Making good quality, visual presentations using Keynote.

- Parallel parking on a busy road.

- Producing words at the drop of a hat when a draft is needed.

Keep listing things, even if you doubt it is a talent. Also list the things you love doing, regardless of your competence.

I love doing...

Where Does Your Talent Shine?

Look at the list of talents you jotted down and have a think about **where you would have to be** for that talent to shine. Write it down next to the list above. You may get an insight about a move you need to make.

Pulling New Talent Out Of You

What scares you? What scares you *and* might help you discover a new talent?

For example:

- Speaking in front of a large crowd scares me but I might discover I enjoy it.

- Being elected to a responsible office scares me but I wonder if I might like the challenge.

- The idea of having children scares me but I could be good at helping them be creative.

Get the idea? Make a list now of things that scare you, that might lie in the future and could help you unlock new talents. What lies in your future that might be the making of you?

Things that scare me but might unlock a talent...

Download The Workbook

At *www.firstknowwhatyouwant.com* you can find your **'First Know Journal'** to print and use with these exercises. Print it as many times as you like and share with friends.

Step 7: The Power Of Keeping Score

So far...

We've started practising by repeatedly making lots of small decisions **(Step 1)** and we've learned how to take what we don't want and reverse it in a way that reveals what we do want **(Step 4)**. If you've started a bug list **(Step 3)** you are already experiencing the relief that comes from keeping promises that you make yourself. And we've been honest with ourselves about how willing we are to turn our wishes or long held dreams into reality **(Step 5)**.

Now we're going to look at another way of discovering what we want – the power of keeping score

How Excited Are You, Right Now?

How excited are you right now?

Too weird? Be playful for a second and answer it for real – if 1/10 was sleepy and 10/10 was firing on all cylinders then, out of 10, right *now*, how excited are you?

Got that? Notice what happens when I ask you to turn it down a bit.

Can you drop your excitement down one level?

What about raising it? Can you increase your excitement by imagining it?

Some people find it helpful to visualise a lever or dial or Star Trek slider.

If you've read this far and haven't done this yet then go back to the top of the page and start again – otherwise everything that follows will just waste your time.

What Happened?

I'm not in the room with you and I don't know you but when I asked you to rate your excitement out of 10 you were able to do it. How?

Thinking (like lightning) you imagined peak excitement for you (10/10) and made an internal comparison to give yourself a rating. Then when I asked you to lower your excitement you were able to do this. You were also able to raise your excitement level just by thinking about it.

With practice you will get good at this. Imagine being able to change your passion level just by imagining a slider or a dial – can you think of any situations where it might be useful to be able to do this?

Using Scales To Know What You Want

Take a look at the diagram below. It's a wheel divided into segments – The Wheel Of Life. Each segment is an area of your life – health, business/career, relationships, personal growth, contribution, etc.

Wheel of Life

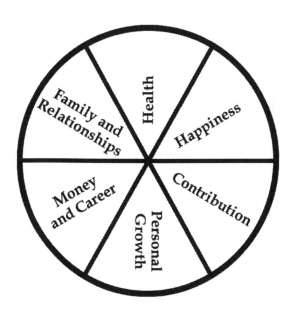

Let's start with the **Health** segment. Thinking about your health and fitness, what would 10/10 be like? If you were rating your health and fitness at 10/10, how would your body feel? What would you see in the mirror? what would you say to yourself? What would others say to you?

Got that?

Now, rate your current level of health and fitness compared to this? Mark it on the wheel and colour in the segment.

Before we leave the health segment, can you think of one small action you could take that would move you closer to 10/10? Write it down.

Do the same, now, for the other five segments – get a clear sense of what 10/10 is, rate your current level, colour in the wheel and write down a small action to move you nearer 10/10.

What Kind Of Wheel Do You Have?

If you rated all your segments the same, say 5/10, then you have a perfect circle coloured in and your life turns smoothly.

If not, imagine trying to drive your car with wheels of the shape you have drawn. Not smooth circles but a bumpy lurch from one thing to another – is this the life you experience?

Two things have just happened. First you have drawn an accurate picture of how you experience life at the moment and second you have a list of six small actions that will change this picture.

Under-Perform To Pick Up Speed

Have you ever had a tyre changed? How do they balance it?

They spin the wheel to see if it runs true. Often a wheel isn't true so they add weights to the rim until they have a perfectly balanced wheel. Why? Because it means you'll go faster and your tyres will last much longer.

In the same way you'll need to add weight to some areas of your life and under-perform in others. Your aim here is to get your life running true. Why? Because *then* you can go much faster and you will last a lot longer.

Look at your extreme scores – the highest compared to the lowest. Here you can see one area of your life that gets too much focus (work?) and another that does not get enough (health?).

The aim here is NOT to rush around madly trying to get each area of life to 10/10. That's too exhausting. What you want is the whole thing to run more smoothly. This means rebalancing all the parts until you would more or less rate them the same – even if that same is only 3/10.

This means you're going to have to under perform in some areas of your life so that you can free up some time and attention for the areas that will bring your life back into balance.

Once you have a wheel that turns smoothly you will be able to pick up speed and move all areas nearer 10/10. But if your diagram is bumpy, this is almost impossible.

Balance first, speed last.

Six Wants

The six small actions you've identified represent six intuitive wants spread across the whole of your life. Combine these now with the previous exercises to make these wishes come true. Find a piece of something that is small enough for you to virtually guarantee you will do it. Do it. Then pick the next one. And so on.

The exercise has some extra tips.

Other Ways To Use The Power Of Keeping Score

Here are some other ways to use scales or scoring systems – with yourself, with those around you and the people you work with.

Using Scales To Coach Yourself

The imaginative use of scales or scoring systems can make a big difference in helping you to uncover or bring to the surface things you want but are not yet fully aware of. You can combine this with the question *What do I want instead?* Use it to manage stress...

I'm sitting in traffic, again, and getting frustrated, again. My shoulders are tense. I'm running disaster scenarios in my head about how late I'm going to be. I'm fuming. I'm swearing that from now on I'll always use trains. My internal dialogue is running at 100mph even if the traffic isn't.

Next time this happens to you, **STOP**. Ask yourself *OK, out of 10 how tense am I?* About 7?

So, what do I want instead?

*I want to be calmer and thinking about something useful, as there is nothing I can actually do about this traffic. I need to think about what I **CAN** do rather than what I can't do.*

Notice something interesting happens. Just by asking the question the tension begins to ease.

The same thing can happen in a boring meeting.

Out of 10 how bored am I right now?

Say 8 out of 10. What would it take to reduce this to 3 or 4? Just asking the question will change how you feel and if you then go on to actually take some action that's even better.

Using Scales To Coach Others

It can work well with children, partners, your boss, friends as well, although I caution you against over using it.

Dad I've got a headache.

Really? If 10/10 was your head exploding all over the room then how bad is your head out of 10?

Depending on your relationship with your kids, this will either get you one of "those looks" or a sensible answer but I promise you the headache will begin to get better.

When your boss hits on you with an urgent problem. Ask them to rate it out of 10. It may calm them down a bit and it may help both of you to understand how important this problem or task or issue actually is.

If your partner is in a state about something, gently, ask them to rate it out of 10 and then what needs doing to improve the score.

Using Scales Of Time And Money

There are other scales you can use too, like time and money. Here are some examples:

Time

- *How important will this seem in five years time?*

- *If we fast forward five years, where or how would you like this to be?*

- *If you carry on like this and nothing changes, where will you be next year or in five years?*

- *Rate yourself now compared to where you were a year ago. Compare yourself to yourself.*

Money

- *How much is this worth to you?*

- *Is this important enough to invest everything you own in it? If not, how important is it?*

Using Scales With People Who Work For You

Scales can be a helpful coaching or management tool because they are so good at surfacing assumptions. Try asking each member of your team, individually, what 10/10 customer service would look and feel like. It's eye opening.

Each person is working to a different assumption. You can show them this effect in a meeting with a simple exercise.

Ask everyone to close their eyes. Then with their eyes still closed, ask them to point to where they think North is. Now, ask them to open their eyes and look around without moving their arms. You will have a room full of people pointing in different directions.

Everyone has a different view of where North is and what *March North* means.

As you know, managing people is not as simple as *March North*. Why? Because there are so many different inter-pretations of where North is. If a group has such differ-ing assumptions about a simple idea like this, imagine the complexity caused by an idea like 'excellent customer service' or 'user friendly website'.

You may well have a team merrily working away to deliver excellent customer service each working to a different set of internal assumptions and a different set of standards.

Ask them to describe what 10/10 is. Ask them where they think they are now. Ask them to think of real actions to bridge the gap. Share your idea of 10/10. Ask them to rate the team performance now. Make a list of actions to bridge the gap.

This is a real, practical way of helping teams know what they want. (And, of course, helping you, the boss, get clear on what you want).

Exercise: The Power Of Keeping Score

Identify the gap between where you are now and where you would like to be. Use this to prompt some small actions to bring your whole life back in balance.

How To Use The Exercise

Start by colouring the squares beside the title in each area to show your score. Draw it as a Wheel Of Life if you like.

Now for each area,

- Build a picture of what 10/10 means for you.

- What will you see when you have this area of your life at 10/10?

- What will you hear others saying or be saying to yourself?

- How will you feel?

If you know what 10/10 is and you know where you are now, then you can begin to think of some of the things you want to do to change or improve this area of your life.

So, **what is one thing you can do, starting now, to improve your score?**

Money & Career	1	2	3	4	5	6	7	8	9	10
What would 10/10 be like?										
What will I see?										
What will I hear?										
What will I feel?										
What is one thing I can do to improve my score?										

Family & Relationships	1	2	3	4	5	6	7	8	9	10
What would 10/10 be like?										
What will I see?										
What will I hear?										
What will I feel?										
What is one thing I can do to improve my score?										

Happiness	1	2	3	4	5	6	7	8	9	10
What would 10/10 be like?										
What will I see?										
What will I hear?										
What will I feel?										
What is one thing I can do to improve my score?										

Personal Growth	1	2	3	4	5	6	7	8	9	10
What would 10/10 be like?										
What will I see?										
What will I hear?										
What will I feel?										
What is one thing I can do to improve my score?										

Health	1	2	3	4	5	6	7	8	9	10
What would 10/10 be like?										
What will I see?										
What will I hear?										
What will I feel?										
What is one thing I can do to improve my score?										

Contribution	1	2	3	4	5	6	7	8	9	10
What would 10/10 be like?										
What will I see?										
What will I hear?										
What will I feel?										
What is one thing I can do to improve my score?										

Six Wants To Move You Forward

This should give you six straightforward actions that cover all the areas of your life, things that you want to happen, desires for each of those areas.

Look to bring your life into balance by getting to roughly equal scores across the whole wheel of life. If your Career/Job score is 7 while Health/Fitness is 3 then you might have to ease back on the Career/Job to pay more attention to Health/Fitness for a while and bring your life into balance.

A smoother wheel of life will run faster than a bumpy one allowing you to get more done, more quickly.

Download The Workbook

At *www.firstknowwhatyouwant.com* you can find your **'First Know Journal'** to print and use with these exercises. Print it as many times as you like and share with friends.

Quick Read: The Power Of Keeping Score

Using scales uncovers hidden assumptions.

If I ask you to rate your health and fitness out of 10, you will consider previously unacknowledged assumptions about what peak health and fitness mean to you. Each of us carries about in our head an ideal marriage, an ideal family, an ideal job, an ideal health and fitness level etc. And we are constantly comparing where we are now to this ideal. You may not have even noticed yourself doing this. By asking you to use a scale I'm now asking you to make the ideal more obvious and the comparison more obvious.

This may have several effects. First it may awaken a desire in you to make progress from where you are now. You may find your ideal compelling and being asked to identify a starting action may nudge you to make progress. It's also possible that you realise your ideal is nonsense and you need a new one. My health and fitness is always going to be 2 out of 10 if I keep comparing myself to Olympic athletes. This is not motivating as I have no realistic hope of attaining 10/10 against this standard. Making this obvious to myself means that I'm likely to choose a more obtainable 10/10 and almost without knowing it I have begun to know more clearly what I want in this part of my life.

Key Points: The Power Of Keeping Score

- We often torture ourselves by comparing our current situation to an impossible standard.

- Stop doing this.

- Get clear on what 10/10 is and then rate your situation against it. Think of small steps that would take you towards 10/10. Start now.

- Aim for a faster turning wheel of life. Balance your wheel so you can pick up speed.

Step 8: Clear The Decks
So Inspiration Can Land

Making room for inspiration

Sometimes inspiration can't land because there's too much stuff in the way. Inspiration is a delicate, flighty creature who is likely to stay away if she sees too much clutter.

We've already seen that physical clutter and unfinished projects represent mental clutter and drain mental energy from you; energy that you could use to create a different future. Having a good clear out will free your time and free mental space for inspiration to land. And you will gain significantly more physical and mental energy.

The Extra Energy Checklist

If you want significantly more physical and mental energy then set to work. The more extreme you are with this, the better your results will be.

Remember:

- If in doubt, chuck it out (apart from essential papers).

- If you've not used it in a year then you're never going to – move it on.

- New things will come when you make room for them.

Everything that is incomplete drains energy from you and from your success. All incomplete things drain energy from your purpose.

- Make a giant **To Do list.** Your aim here is to get it all out of your head. Use one card or slip of paper per item so they are easier to sort. Start every day with a list of things todo and cross it off as you go. At least once a week, sort through ALL your jobs and plan for the coming week.

- Put all your appointments in a **calendar** – get them out of your email. Refer to it daily. Plan your time. Stick to it.

- **Clean up your house, and/or your office.** Imagine an important visitor was coming who you wanted to impress. Clean up for yourself as if you were that important visitor. Clean your work area, sharpen your pencils, get rid of old stuff lying around.

- **Clean up your car** – inside and out. Get it serviced.

- **Organise** all your papers. Throw away everything you don't use, haven't used in six months, or which is outdated. Keep and file all business receipts, essential papers (tax; chequebooks, statements etc)

- **Clean out all filing cabinets.**

- **Clean off the top of your desk.**

- **Get your chequebook balanced.**

- Get all **financial statements** (Profit & Loss and Balance Sheet) up to date. Keep them up to date. You need to know where you are with money. It only works for you if you pay attention to it.

- **Pay all your bills** or arrange/agree when you will pay them. Keep those agreements.

- Make a list of **everyone who owes you money,** or who has borrowed things. Write or call and ask for the money (or the thing borrowed), or cross the person off the list and decide it is complete.

- Make a list of all the things you have **started but not completed.** Complete the list, or cross it off and decide not to do it, eg DIY jobs that are 95% done. Do the last 5% or they will continue to suck energy from you.

- Make a list of all the things you have started, are ongoing, and which are incomplete. Complete the list, or cross it off and decide not to do it.

- Make a list of all the things which have been going on a long time but you have just not completed. Complete the list or cross it off and decide not to do it.

- Make a list of all the **agreements** you've made. Fulfill all past agreements. Renegotiate and make new agreements with any that you that can't fulfill.

- **Take total responsibility for your results.** From now on, only say Yes to something you know you can do. Do only what you can, delegate the rest. Never commit to more than you know you can do. Only make promises you can keep.

- Pick one small thing you could do to take care of your physical body and start doing it. Build a new habit.

You Wear Your Insides, Outside

Want to know what's going on inside? Take a look around you. Your car is a mess and needs repairing. You're hanging on to a lot of old junk. You owe money. People owe you.

What you're seeing is the reality of your state of mind. We tend to create circumstances that reflect what's going on inside and these are like unconscious signals for those who can read them. This is why, for example, people with low self esteem often have poor personal grooming and wear scruffy clothes. They are signalling what's going on. It's why teenagers with low body confidence hide in baggy clothing to protect themselves – they feel vulnerable.

This works both ways. Internal changes will show externally in your life and you can also make internal changes by working on the external stuff. By clearing up around you, by straightening up and getting rid of old baggage you'll experience a leap in mental clarity too. You can loosen mental congestion by getting rid of physical congestion. Holding onto old stuff is a signal that you are holding onto old ideas that are no longer useful.

You wear your insides, outside.

Clutter, mess and unfinished business are depressing and act as a mental brake. Straighten out one and you tend to straighten out the other. Remember that your surroundings signal to the world around you – what signal are you sending? Everything around you is there with your permission. It remains there with your permission.

And as a nice bonus, after clearing the decks you will feel noticeably better too.

What About The In-Between Stuff?

You know the 'in-between' stuff. Not clear that you should get rid of it and not clear that you should keep it? It's the stuff that makes you dither or feel uncertain. It might be useful one day. The reality is that you should only hang on to stuff you are clear about. As you probably realise by now, if you are dithering about a lot of stuff; it's an accurate reflection of other things you dither about too.

Put the in-between stuff in a box. Seal it. Label it with a date six months from now. If it helps, put a note inside about the thing you are dithering about (you know what it is).

If you break the seal in the next six months then it's probably something useful and you should keep it. If the box is still sealed then go ahead and move this clutter along. You no longer need it. Give it away or turn it back into money by selling it. Use the money to create the life you want.

By deliberately reducing the amount of stuff you are uncertain about, you deliberately reduce the amount of internal uncertainty you have. And you gain clarity – knowing more clearly what you want to keep in your life.

Key Points: Clear The Decks

- Look around you. Whatever you think, you are what you do.

- You build your outsides to show off your insides. Confused and messy outside usually indicates confused thinking inside.

- By changing the outside you can change the inside.

- As you clear the decks, you create space for inspiration to land.

Step 9: Live Now!

In which we learn to live now.

So far…

As you start to use scales with others you'll notice that when you ask them what 10/10 would be, they always know. And getting them to compare their present score with this ideal provokes some sort of action more often than not. It's strange but you can have a lot of fun with it **(Step 7)**.

Releasing clutter is fun too and it's amazing how creating physical space frees up your thinking **(Step 8)**. Let's look now at what else you might want to do.

Working Backwards From The End

At what time, in most people's lives, do they realise they might have some regrets about missed opportunities?

Towards the end of life, when they are old or sick or both. By then, of course, it is probably too late. It's ironic. At the end of your life you finally have the free time you've been waiting for but lack the energy or money to do anything with it. The time to consider these things is **now**, while you can still do something about it.

The average lifespan for a man in the UK is 80. For a woman, 85. You can work out for yourself the average amount of years you have left. What do you want to do with the time remaining?

Consider the questions below and as you do let the answers bubble up from inside you. Hold back on any judgement about whether what you want is realistic or not. Let it come.

Who Would You Like To Meet?

Is there anybody who you would love to meet or talk to before you end your time on earth? Who?

Where Would You Like To Go?

Places to visit, things to see for yourself.

Is There Anything You Would Love To Learn Or Achieve?

Perhaps you have always nursed a desire to fly helicopters or play the piano or finally master a Rubiks Cube.

What Experiences Would You Like To Have?

Our world offers a wealth of experiences. You can do anything, anywhere. Is there anything you would like to experience before you are too feeble to do anything about it?

What Things Would You Like To Own?

If you could pick a toy to have or treasured possession, what would it be?

And When You Are Gone?

And the last thing to think about is your legacy, what would you like to *leave behind you* when you go from here? Or put another way, what *contribution* do you want to make to the world? If any?

One of the strangest thing about our perspective on life is that we constantly misjudge what is possible. We overestimate what we can do in a day but underestimate what we can do in a year.

Take learning a new language as an example. Rush at it, trying to cram learning into a few weeks, and you will get disillusioned but learn a verb a day for 365 days and your progress will astound you.

The time you have left is both a long time and a short time. It's long enough to achieve almost anything but short enough to remind you to start *now* before it drains away.

Almost anything is possible if you spread it out over this time. If you've nursed a desire to see the Grand Canyon then why not make a plan to see it in five years and start moving towards it now? Same with your helicopter idea. It may seem daunting and unobtainable now but broken down into little pieces, you easily have the time.

Where Do I Find The Money To Do What I Want?

What stops many of these plans is thinking about how much they will cost and then thinking that you will do them once you retire and are living on a pension or your investments.

Hmm. Do you know what Albert Einstein called the most powerful force in the universe? **It's the power of compound interest.** Look it up. Compound interest means that for the price of the money you fritter on regular album downloads, you could easily have a Grand Canyon holiday in a few years.

Remember when we talked about turning wishes into reality. If you want it you can start taking small actions now to have it happen in the future.

Every week or every day you get to decide – do I want this new album or do I want that trip? Sometimes you can have both, sometimes you need to make a choice.

Exercise: Live Now

Death, eh? Comes to us all eventually. How would you like to use the time before you get there?

How To Use The Exercise

Subtract your age now from the average life expectancy for a man (80) and woman (85). This gives you your remaining years. Now use the Exercise to consider what you want before it is too late.

	Man	Woman
Average lifespan:	80	85
My age now:		
Average number of years left to me:		

As you work through these questions forget about being realistic or practical. Just capture your first thoughts.

- What are some of the things you *want* to do in the time remaining to you?

- What *should* you do?

- What do you *feel compelled* to do?

- What do you *just have* to do?

- What places do you *need* to visit? What experiences do you need to have?

- Who would you like to *meet* in the time remaining?

- Where would you like to *go*? What would you like to *see*?

- Is there anything you would love to *learn or achieve* in this time?

- What would you love to *create*?

- What *experiences* would you like to have?

- What things would you like to *own*?

- And the last thing to think about is your legacy, what would you like to *leave behind* you when you go from here? Or put another way, what *contribution* do you want to make to the world? If any?

- Most people have something they want to do before they die – what is it for you?

Area	Ideas
People I want to meet	
Places I want to go	
Experiences I want to have	
Things I want to learn	
Contribution I want to make	

Then ask yourself *why*? What would this bring you?

How else could you achieve it? Fill the boxes with your desires and all the ways you could achieve the same result.

Write it down. Now.

If you're still coming up blank, then start with *one thing*.

- What is *one thing* you want to do before you die?

- Which *one place* do you want to visit?

- Name *one experience* you would like to have?

- Suggest *one thing* you would like to create?

And so on…

Beginning To Make It Happen

Use the process from **Step 5** to pick two or three small actions you can take now to move you closer to these goals. For example you may not be able to book your dream holiday now but you can easily open a savings account and start putting in small regular payments.

Download The Workbook

At *www.firstknowwhatyouwant.com* you can find your **'First Know Journal'** to print and use with these exercises. Print it as many times as you like and share with friends.

Quick Read: Live Now

We mostly avoid talking about death and forget that we are all going to get old someday and leave the planet. Wouldn't it be wonderful to look back on a life where you did the things you were interested in and left some contribution that you could be proud of? Why not choose to live *now*?

Step 9 works by challenging the widely held assumption that you can postpone your real life until some later point. 80 years is not long and it's one heck of a gamble to save up all the things you want to do until some mythical point in the future when you think opportunity will smile on you.

Think about them now. People, travel, toys, experiences, learning and contribution. What are those things that you feel compelled to do while you are here on the earth?

If you could make sure that you did just one thing before you left this planet, what would that one thing be?

Remember the old saying, it's a rare man who gets to the end of his life and wishes he'd spent *more* time in the office or commuting or in meetings. Wouldn't it be great if there were few things you wished you'd spent more time doing because you spread them out across your life?

Would You Have Eaten The Marshmallow?

Have you heard about the marshmallow test?

Apparently a group of researchers were looking for a way of working out which children would be successful later in life. They had a theory that people who were able to defer an immediate gain for a later one would be better at working towards future success rather than settling for an easy win. So they came up with the marshmallow test.

They put a marshmallow in front of a child and told them that if they waited until the researcher came back they could have a second one but if they ate it now they wouldn't get a second one.

And you can guess the end of the story. When they followed up years later they found that the children who had waited 10 minutes for the second marshmallow were much better at working towards a gain in the future rather than taking a gain now.

Live Now

While this may be true, we only have a short time and our challenge is not to defer the gain so long we never actually do it. Remembering to take time with others, to balance your life properly, even to plan your weekends are all things to do now, whilst also saving towards making sure you have both the time and money to do the bigger things as well.

We tend to overestimate what we can do in a day, and underestimate what we can do in a year.

Key Points: Live Now

- Live now. TV companies want you sitting in drugged immobility so that they can sell you stuff. Instead of sitting there watching pretend lives, turn it off and go and get one of your own.

- Use the energy you have now to live a more interesting life now.

- You can do more in a year than you believe possible.

- Whatever you think, plan or dream, your life is what you actually do. What are you doing in the next seven days to live now?

Step 10: Stop Thinking
And Come To Your Senses

In which we learn the power of paying attention to our senses.

This one is easy...

Where are you and what are you doing when your senses come alive?

Look around you now. Let me ask you some strange questions about your environment. Answer them as honestly as you can (but you don't have to talk out loud!).

- What can you smell right now? They say that after you've worked in a cheese factory for a while you can no longer smell the cheese. Which smells have you tuned out from your immediate environment?

- What can you hear? Take a moment to isolate all the different sounds, including your own breathing.

- What can you feel on your body? Your watch maybe, your clothes. Touch a few of the different textures near you to get a sense of the variety.

- And lastly, what do you see right now. Look around and do yourself a little running commentary on what you can see.

Got all that? Would you say you are in a highly stimulating environment that encourages your creativity? Let me tell you what the latest brain research shows.

The Brain Dead Primates

You might have heard the story that when we get to a certain age our brain cells start to die off? Well, it turns out that it's not true.

The original brain research which led to this 'fact' was done with primates and of course the primates were kept in an artificial environment, breathing recycled air, in steel coloured cages, set against white painted walls. It's no surprise that their brain cells started to die off.

Just recently a group of researchers discovered that if you took the same primates and put them in a highly stimulating, natural setting, which fired their senses, guess what? Their brain cells started regrowing and not just growing but stretching and making new connections. Can you see a link here?

The same thing happens to us. Put a young human in a sensory deprived environment (like most workplaces) and the only way their brains survive is because they are released at the end of each day and get a couple of days off a week. It's urgent that you stimulate your senses if you want to make new connections and prevent unnecessary brain cell death.

Stop Thinking And Come to Your Senses

I don't want you to think about this at all. All I want you to do is pay attention to what your senses are telling you and especially what your senses long for more of. Most people who work in an artificial environment are so disconnected from their senses that it takes ages before they become aware of what they are sensing.

Many people have gone numb. Think about those who work in any sort of factory or corporate environment. The colours are dull and muted, usually a variety of grey, beige, white or blue. They only ever write with blue or black ink on white paper. In more physical environments the noise can be relentless and the activity repetitive. No wonder we go numb.

Grandma Is Fat

We also go numb on how we feel and think. Just the other day, my family were all sitting having dinner when my youngest blurted out *'Grandma is fat isn't she?'* She's six and she just blurted it out in the middle of everything else because it came into her head. You used to do this kind of thing but you don't anymore, do you?

Your parents or some authority figure soon told you that it was not good to speak your thoughts. Of course, this makes sense. We'd have anarchy if everyone just said whatever they were thinking from moment to moment. Most relationships would not last long if this was the case.

It does have a downside though. If you are constantly shushing yourself, constantly telling yourself that you are not allowed to think or say a particular thought then after a while you lose contact with what you think. All of us have had the experience of adopting a bland persona at work. Unfortunately, in many places you soon learn that original thought is neither desired nor welcome. You are careful never to express a view in a meeting, never to hold a strong opinion. You see that convention and conformity are the keys to promotion. Again, after a few years of this, it can be hard to find any kind of originality or definite thought in you at all.

Stay In Touch With Your Senses

If this hasn't happened to you yet then can I plead with you to stay in touch with the information from your senses because it gives you some kind of grounding for knowing who you are in the world and what you want and enjoy. Stop thinking and come to what your senses are telling you.

Part of figuring out what you want this way is to understand what you take pleasure in and rediscover the deep longings you have to satisfy those senses. Let me ask you a few questions about your senses and what they are telling you.

Sight

- What do you most enjoy looking at?

- What would you like to view more regularly?

- What brings delight to your eyes?

- How could you see and experience that more often?

Sound

- What is your favourite sound, noise, music etc?

- What would you like to hear more often?

In one workshop, a lady told me that her favourite sound was laughter. *How much laughter do you hear where you work now?* I asked. *Not much* was the answer.

Why aren't all our workplaces filled with laughter?

Touch

- What do you like to touch or feel?

- Who or what do you like to touch?

- Who or what do you like to be touched by?

No sniggers please. Research has shown that touch is one of the best ways to banish loneliness and depression in the elderly. We hug and carry children a lot because we know touch is one of the best ways to reassure them. We seem to forget that with adults. In some societies and cultures the whole touching thing has become a minefield, laden with threats of legal action and overtones of exploitation. None of that changes our need for a hug though.

So, what surfaces, textures, items or who do you love to touch or be touched by?

How easy would you find it just to bring back some lovely textures into your working day, perhaps a new scarf or the feeling of a fountain pen on nice paper.

Smell

- What is your favourite smell?

- How often do you get to smell your favourite smell?

- How could you smell it more often?

- How could you stay in touch with those smells?

133

It's so important, especially if you have been breathing air conditioned or recycled air all day at work. Smell connects us directly to our most ancient memories. On parents evening, that school smell is way too close for comfort!

Taste

- Favourite tastes, then. What are they and how could you taste them more often?

Taste is the sense that most accurately tells us whether we have become bland or numb to our world. If you find yourself having to add loads of salt to your food to get it to taste of anything then it may be a sign of stress. I know when I'm stressed because I start pouring chilli sauce and mustard on my food. Anything to get any kind of flavour.

I have no real evidence for this but I'm not the only one who begins to lose my sense of taste when stressed or tense. If you are numbing out your senses on caffeine or desperately craving the sugary or salty high of junk food it could be that you have become totally disconnected from your taste buds. And, of course, that physical disconnection is a sure sign of mental disconnection. To combat your stress, bland or numb feelings, bring your senses back.

Just concentrate on what your senses are telling you – what do you want more of and how could you bring these things back into your life? Oh and why not hold your next team meeting in the park?

Exercise: Stop Thinking
And Come To Your Senses

Five senses. Sight, Sound, Touch, Smell and Taste. If, through stress or lack of practice, you are numb to sensual pleasure, please indulge yourself with these questions to discover what you want more of.

How To Use The Exercise

Come to your senses. Just answer the questions.

Senses	More...
I most love LOOKING at:	How can I SEE more?
I most love TOUCHING:	How can I FEEL more?
I most like to be TOUCHED:	How can I have this more often?
I most love TASTING:	How can I TASTE more?
I most love HEARING:	How can I HEAR more?
I most love SMELLING:	How can I SMELL more?

What would I do on a weekend spent pleasuring my senses?

How can I make my workplace more sensual? – think about texture, colour, nature, even smells and tastes.

Bring Your Senses Back To Life

Many of these are small, easy changes you can build into your day. You want them and they bring you pleasure. Get to it.

Download The Workbook

At *www.firstknowwhatyouwant.com* you can find your **'First Know Journal'** to print and use with these exercises. Print it as many times as you like and share with friends.

Quick Read: Stop Thinking And Come To Your Senses

To be more sensual, slow down.

Often we numb or ignore our senses because we are moving through our lives too fast and it is annoying to have to slow down and pay attention to them. It is a bit like taking a toddler for a walk. The child keeps wanting to go in different directions and stopping to investigate interesting things.

Hurry up, hurry up, you cry to your senses, pulling on the leash. It's no wonder they stop talking to you after a while.

So slow down. Pay attention.

- What are your senses telling you that you want?

- Are your senses fulfilled by the way you live at the moment, are you a sensual person?

- Did you find that question threatening or disturbing? If you did, what do you want instead?

- What are your senses telling you about what you want?

Tips For Developing Your Senses

Here are a few ideas for stimulating or recovering contact with your senses which might help you get back in touch.

Some of them seem silly and they won't all help but, hey, have a go anyway...

- Look at the pens you normally use. Decide to write in a non standard colour all day – green, red, purple, brown.

- Retune your car radio to a different channel for a week. If you listen mainly to speech then tune to music or a foreign language station. If you listen mainly to music then choose a different type of music.

- Spend half hour at the perfume counter in a big store trying out new scents.

- Close your eyes with the first mouthful of food or first sip of wine. Concentrate on the flavours and smell.

- Touch everything in your working environment slowly and deliberately. Make a decision about whether you like it or not.

- Treat yourself to a small sensual treat which you can enjoy, some quality paper to write on, a new pen, a silk scarf, an expensive ice cream. Anything that will reconnect you with your senses.

- Consider playing with a sensual activity – music, dance, poetry, drawing, painting, sculpture, even a DIY project or washing the car. Just pick something that gets you out of your head and using your body.

Key Points: Come To Your Senses

- If 1/10 was totally numb and 10/10 was all senses firing then how alive are you, right now, to your senses?

- What do you want to touch, taste, smell, hear or look at that would help you live again?

- Go do it.

Step 11: Uncover Your Values

The secret to knowing what you want is knowing who you are. Have you every felt out of step with the people around you? That somehow they all seem fine but you feel that you don't quite fit? Has it ever become obvious that you see the world in a different way to those nearby?

What you're experiencing is a clash of values, a disconnection between what you think is important and what they think is important.

What Are Values?

Values are the things that drive you, the things that tell you what is important in a given situation.

For example, if I asked you what is important to you about your relationships at work, you might say Kindness or Laughter or Intellectual Stimulation. I would get different answers from everyone I asked and you would probably have more than one thing that's important – you have a list.

These are your values, your unconscious drivers. If you place a high value on Kindness you will use this to sort out in your own mind whether you are in the right place or not. It will also drive you to find a place where you experience Kindness.

Where Do Your Values Come From?

Some say that your values form quite quickly, around the time of puberty and from then on they are pretty much fixed unless you make a deliberate effort to change them. You might like to cast your mind back to what was happening when you were around 12 because that's when your values started to form.

At that age you began to come to some conclusions about work, relationships, family life etc. and those conclusions have been part of your driving force ever since.

How Your Values Can Help You Know What You Want

Uncovering or remembering your values can help you decide what you want because they remind you of what you believe to be truly important about each area of your life. In the general busyness of growing up, finding work and establishing relationships we can sometimes forget what our values are.

It's only after being in a situation for a while that we begin to notice something not quite right. Maybe a little free floating anxiety, maybe a feeling of disconnection from the people around you or maybe just the sense that you don't quite fit somehow. These are often the result of a clash between what you are doing and what your true internal drivers are, the behaviour you believe is important.

The other confusing thing about your values is that you've got them arranged in a hierarchy and it may be that your current situation meets some of your values but not all of them. I see this a lot in clients who know that what they are doing isn't working. Their problem is since that it works a bit and is not bad enough to do anything about, they never make the changes they need to make.

Take my example of relationships at work (above). Let's say Kindness is number three on your list. It's the third most important thing about relationships at work. If your work relationships satisfy your top two values but not the third then you'll find yourself in this state. Your relationships at work don't feel quite right but neither are they bad enough to do anything about. This does not provide enough of a push to do anything about but leaves you in a kind of limbo where you are not quite there. You might experience this as something you can't quite put your finger on.

What helps in all these cases is to bring your values to the front of your mind. Write them down and then take a good look at whether you are acting in line with what you believe to be truly important.

Do It Soon

It's much easier to find a workplace that fits your values than to change your values to suit the place you earn a living. In fact, constantly having to compromise your values can eventually make you quite ill.

If there is a difference between what you value and where you are or what you are doing, you'll find that life has a way of reminding you of this. It continually throws up opportunities to look again at your values by changes like settling down with a partner, having children, economic challenges etc. Even with this help though many people put up with years of disparity between what they value and what they are actually doing. Then it explodes in a mid-life crisis or dramatic relationship change or similar.

Why wait until changes are dramatic and painful? Uncover your values now by reminding yourself of what you truly find important. Begin, now, to make the small changes that brings your life closer to reflecting what you value.

Exercise: Uncover Your Values

Step 1: Pick an area of your life where you would like to understand your values: eg *Work*

Step 2: Make sure you've chosen the right word for the area you picked: Work or Job or Career or Role or Business. Got that?

Step 3: Now ask yourself *What is important to me about Work?* and write down all the words that spring to mind until you have a list of 8 – 10 concepts. Your list will vary but it might include things like challenge, opportunity, variety, laughter etc.

Step 4: Look at your list and find the most important value. The one you would choose above all the others. Write it down at the top of a new list. Continue down with the second most important and so on. Group similar terms and if you are stuck between two, force yourself to choose.

Step 5: Now rate your situation against your topmost value. For example, if you said that *challenge* is the most important thing about **Work** then score your current situation out of 10 with 10/10 indicating that value is totally satisfied at work. Continue down the list.

Step 6: What have you learned? You can see why you feel about **Work** the way you do.

Using What You Value

Once you understand your particular list of values for **Work**, you'll see that some are satisfied and some are not. The best place for you to work is a place that satisfies your top three values. That's a place where the work you do is a perfect fit with the work values that drive you – the things that are most important to you.

I've used **Work** as an example here and I suggest that you repeat the exercise for all the significant parts of your life.

Uncover your values for your Wheel of Life:

- Your health and fitness
- Your relationship
- Your finances
- Your leisure time
- Your contribution / legacy
- Your spiritual life

Knowing these helps you know who you are and what you want. You might like to begin thinking of some practical ways you could start to change your situation so that there is a better fit with what you believe is truly important.

Key Points: Uncover Your Values

- For every area of your life you have a list of what is most important to you – what you value.

- These values are your unconscious drivers and you will feel a constant push to satisfy them.

- Staying where your values are not satisfied will disturb you. Either your situation or what you believe is important will have to change.

- It's important to understand what your values are (you may be unaware) because that may help you understand changes you need to make.

- The secret of knowing what you want is knowing who you are.

Step 12: Follow Your Joy

In which we learn to find nuggets in the dirt.

So far…

Perhaps you have begun to experiment with keeping your senses alive at home and at work **(Step 10)**. Eating more slowly to see whether you can taste your food. Putting more plants in the office. Breathing in strongly to fill your lungs with fresh air when you go outside. Learning the benefits of being surrounded by nature while you talk. You've also done some work on your values and realised what is important to you **(Step 11)**.

Now let's look at how a polar bear can help you discover the place where you belong.

Considering Polar Bears

I remember visiting a big zoo as a child. It wasn't a pleasant experience. There was a polar bear, alone in a grey concrete enclosure with a scummy moat at the front. This bear was pacing up and down, pausing only to bang its head hard against the wall. Then it would turn, and sway, gently, to the other end where it would bang its head violently against that wall. It had cage fever. Horrible? Yep. Why do I want to remember that?

I keep a toy polar bear on my desk to remind me what they are like in the wild. They play, hunt, run, roll around in snow. Most of all they live joyfully, by polar bear standards at least.

And that's a clue to finding out where you should be, where you fit best and ultimately what you want. Animals in their natural environment are naturally joyful because it suits them, they fit. Look at sparrows hopping about or lions roaming around the plains.

Put an animal in an artificial environment and soon you get deviant, self destructive, behaviour. Caged birds will pull out their own fur, some animals refuse to breed, some engage in meaningless, repetitive actions. They display signs of something close to madness.

Why should it be any different with humans? Take a living, breathing, young person and shut them up away from the sun and rain in a monotone environment with recycled air and what do you get? After a few years they have no possible way of understanding where they naturally *fit*.

Which brings us to the easiest, and the hardest, of all the things we have looked at. Easy because all you have to do is find the place where you are at your most joyful. And it's hard because finding that place is going to take some work and some thinking.

Find A Square Hole

If you are a square peg in a round hole then which is easier – to shave off your corners until you fit or to go and find a square hole?

Naturally, it's easier to find a square hole. But you'd be surprised how tenaciously we cling to the wrong place at the wrong time. In truth, it's quite hard to acknowledge that we are in the wrong place and move somewhere else. We seem programmed to make the best of where we are, scared to do anything else.

I'm just warning you that while this is the easiest of all my suggestions, it's not going to feel like the easiest. In fact it might feel like an awful lot of work.

Approach The Problem Backwards

Consider this. How do you sort out where you fit best? How do you find your square hole, the ideal environment where you are naturally joyful and expressive?

The answer lies in approaching the problem backwards. Instead of racking your brains for inspiration on where you fit best, **take a long look back at the past.** Search hard for all those times when you have been at your most joyful, all those times when it felt just right. Put them all together and see what that tells you about the place, environment or surroundings where you will be at your best.

Time to dig up the past. Use the next exercise to excavate your joy – so you can follow it.

Exercise: Follow Your Joy

This exercise is about finding your joy. Those times when you were absorbed, playful, creative, expressive and pleased with what you did. As you look back over your life and bring these incidents to mind you will be able to see patterns emerging that tell you about the times, circumstances, places and groups where you *fit* best. Where you can be yourself naturally and the work fits you as if it was something you were born to do.

What brought you joy could be anything, of any size. It does not matter whether others would think it significant, only that it gave you joy. It could be a Lego house you built, an exam you passed, learning to drive or just an essay you wrote for history class that you were proud of.

If you are struggling to remember joy, then think of achievements you were proud of. Again, it does not matter whether others noticed, only that you did.

How To Use The Exercise

Start with your early years – between 0-12 years old. Now bring to mind a memory of an achievement that gave you joy. It may have been something as simple as the day you learned to ride a bike or ice skating for the first time or a sandcastle that you built with your dad. You are not looking here for achievements that others would recognise, only achievements that *you* enjoyed and felt good.

Think about this time and the achievement. Then answer the questions...

- What actually happened? Note down the details

- What specifically made it joyful?

- What abilities did you reveal by achieving this?

- What general type or category would you put this in?

- Who else was there? Note any significant people or things

It's important that you write this down, and don't just run it through your mind. The physical movement of writing and the creative act of making marks on paper activate many other useful parts of your mind (and you'll need your notes at the end).

Now repeat for the years 12 to 18. And so on.

When you reach your present age, turn to the summary page to find out how to use this information.

0-12 Years: My Greatest Joy...

Identify an achievement that brought you joy

What actually happened? Note down the details

What specifically made it joyful?

What abilities did you reveal by achieving this?

What general type or category would you put this in?

Who else was there? Note any significant people or things

13-17 Years: My Greatest Joy...

Identify an achievement that brought you joy

What actually happened? Note down the details

What specifically made it joyful?

What abilities did you reveal by achieving this?

What general type or category would you put this in?

Who else was there? Note any significant people or things

18-22 Years: My Greatest Joy…

Identify an achievement that brought you joy

What actually happened? Note down the details

What specifically made it joyful?

What abilities did you reveal by achieving this?

What general type or category would you put this in?

Who else was there? Note any significant people or things

23-30 Years: My Greatest Joy...

Identify an achievement that brought you joy

What actually happened? Note down the details

What specifically made it joyful?

What abilities did you reveal by achieving this?

What general type or category would you put this in?

Who else was there? Note any significant people or things

31-40 Years: My Greatest Joy...

Identify an achievement that brought you joy

What actually happened? Note down the details

What specifically made it joyful?

What abilities did you reveal by achieving this?

What general type or category would you put this in?

Who else was there? Note any significant people or things

41-50 Years: My Greatest Joy...

Identify an achievement that brought you joy

What actually happened? Note down the details

What specifically made it joyful?

What abilities did you reveal by achieving this?

What general type or category would you put this in?

Who else was there? Note any significant people or things

51-60 Years: My Greatest Joy...

Identify an achievement that brought you joy

What actually happened? Note down the details

What specifically made it joyful?

What abilities did you reveal by achieving this?

What general type or category would you put this in?

Who else was there? Note any significant people or things

61-70 Years: My Greatest Joy...

Identify an achievement that brought you joy

What actually happened? Note down the details

What specifically made it joyful?

What abilities did you reveal by achieving this?

What general type or category would you put this in?

Who else was there? Note any significant people or things

70+ Years: My Greatest Joy...

Identify an achievement that brought you joy

What actually happened? Note down the details

What specifically made it joyful?

What abilities did you reveal by achieving this?

What general type or category would you put this in?

Who else was there? Note any significant people or things

When You Followed Your Joy

After you've captured all your memories of achievements that brought you joy, please sum up what you've found with these questions:

1. Throughout your life what type of activity consistently produced the greatest sense of joy?

2. What are you doing that you most like to do? Who are you being when you enjoy it the most?

3. What do you most like about yourself?

4. What patterns and trends do you observe in your answers so far?

5. Now, what action are you going to take so that you do more of what you love?

Download The Workbook

At *www.firstknowwhatyouwant.com* you can find your **'First Know Journal'** to print and use with these exercises. Print it as many times as you like and share with friends.

Quick Read: Follow Your Joy

Cast your mind back across your life and pick a memory of something you enjoyed doing. It can be big or small, doesn't matter. It can be public or private, it can be something you have fond memories of and no one else noticed, it doesn't matter. The only thing that does matter is that you enjoyed it, a lot.

Now as you replay that event or achievement I'm willing to bet that you felt connected, involved, motivated and maybe a sense of achievement? If so you've stumbled across the secret of **Step 12: Follow Your Joy.**

Put simply, you need to track down all these times in your life when you felt like this and then like an archeologist putting all the bones on the same table, work out what this tells you. Having excavated all these joyful achievements, what happens when you assemble them all? What themes or patterns emerge that tell you something about the kind of work, environment and groups where you fit? What kind of creature are you, really?

This can take some work though. It's archeology, remember. A recent client who did this exercise ended up with a list of joyful achievements that was mostly a list of books read, films watched and TV watched. He looked at this list and wailed 'I'm happiest watching television. How will that help me find work that pays the bills and fits my interests?'

Leaving aside all the jobs that *do* involve watching television all day, I did a bit of digging around with him about what it was about TV that he liked. It turned out that it wasn't books, films or TV that were giving him that sense of joy, it was *stories*. He loved stories, reading them, following them, talking about them, being around them. And there are endless jobs and lives that will get you near stories all day.

Once we'd identified his true source of joy it wasn't long before he started planning a life and career change that would put stories at the heart of everything he did.

Excavate your joy, then follow it.

Key Points: Follow Your Joy

- You're not a blank slate. There are places where you fit best and places where you don't. Your joy is the clearest indicator that you've found one. Not fleeting happiness but joy – a deep sense of delight in doing something for it's own sake.

- What do you want? You want to be safe, warm and dry. You want enough variety to spark your interest and help you feel alive. You want to be unique yet connected closely to those you love. And you want to grow and feel that this life has some meaning, you've contributed something.

- How do you get this? By doing more of what gets these results and less of what doesn't.

- Eat more of the food that gives you energy and less of the food that doesn't.

  Result: More energy

- Be with people who energise you and less time with those who drain you.

  Result: More love/connection

- Do more work that sparks your interest and helps you grow. Do less of the work that causes you to shrivel and numb.

  Result: More interesting work and better results

- Notice where you can make a contribution that helps others and brings you joy. Do more of it.

  Result: You've found your slot

- If you're a square peg surrounded by round holes then go find a square hole somewhere. Follow your joy.

- Joy is the clearest indicator of the intersection between what you were built to do and the best place to do it.

Part 5: Get 1% Closer
To What You Want

By now you should be getting at least some inkling of what you want but how do you set out to get it?

Can I suggest a plan? Take baby steps.

Avoid Black And White Thinking

Finally knowing what you want often comes with a rush of clarity and enthusiasm that may surprise you. In all the excitement it's easy to make rash promises to change or say and do things that upset the established order around you. Sometimes this is necessary, but more often than not you can ease your way towards the life you want, taking other people with you.

A common symptom of over enthusiasm is the kind of black and white thinking that makes everything into a dramatic choice, eg I've got to start my own business or I will be stuck in this boring corporate job forever. Caught between choice A or choice B you find yourself on the horns of a dilemma. This approach is nonsense but easy to fall prey too when you get a rush of motivation.

Relationships, jobs and long established behaviours should not be tossed aside lightly. Which means we need an approach to change that gets us moving but allows for a more sober pace. You have more than two choices don't you? In fact there are infinite combinations of A and B along the way to what you want. This means you have almost infinite choices about how to start making the changes you want.

Digital thinking is like a switch with only two options – A, on or B, off. When we fool ourselves into thinking of only two choices we are thinking digital. It's like driving a car that only has two speeds.

Analog thinking is like a dial with infinite possible adjustments between A and B. Real driving gives is an infinite range of speed choices which we adjust constantly. When we realise we have more than two choices it is easier to find something to start with. Here's a suggestion:

Stop, Start, Continue

If your changes are going to stick and you really are going to move towards what you want, then understand that for every gain you make, something or someone will lose something. New things mean destruction of the old order and this is not always comfortable or welcome.

You can break this change down into three main areas – things you start, things you stop and things you continue to do.

Have a go now:

- What do I need to start?
- What do I need to stop?
- What do I need to continue?

Put this together with a timeline and you get a table something like this:

	Now	Later	Future
Start			
Stop			
Continue			

Take a few moments now to plot your changes using this table. Define your own timescale for **Later** and **Future** or leave them undefined.

What you have now is a more measured approach to making the changes you want that will get you nearer to what you want.

Look For 1% Improvements

The quickest way to feel more energetic after meals is to notice which foods give you more energy and eat more of them. Eat less of food that robs you of energy. Even a minor change at every meal would change your life.

Likewise, the quickest way to have what you want is to start making changes today. There's a danger though, that you will a) overestimate how much you can change and b) this thought defeats you before you start.

The solution?

Easy. Look for a 1% change. What could you do today that would get you 1% nearer what you really want? Make it small and do it. Then wait until tomorrow. Tomorrow ask yourself the question again. What would get me 1% nearer my goals? Find it and do it. A week later you will be 7% closer to what you want, a far faster rate of progress than if you had tried to make a 7% change on the first day.

After a month of doing this you will be 30% nearer to what you want. Keep it up for a year and the scale of the changes you have made will astound you.

Use Your Imagination

Creating something new begins with your imagination. Consider the last time you cleaned your teeth. There was a moment, just before you did it, when you experienced it in your imagination first. You imagined how your teeth would feel when they were clean, you heard the sound of the brush or perhaps made a fleeting picture of the bathroom. It happened in your mind first and then you made it happen for real.

Look around you. Every created thing sprung from someone's imagination. Sometimes it forms in your mind so quickly that you do not notice it. At other times it's obvious. All creation echos the original creative act, it starts with imagination, you see it, hear it or sense it and then you make it real.

161

Of course, it's not perfect and you may be bruised from having imagined many things you've failed to create. Maybe you have imagined being a non-smoker but failed to create it or imagined a slimmer you who has yet to emerge. Nonetheless, the only way to have a different future is to form it inside first. Don't wait for evolution, you haven't got time. You're going to have to go with creation and that only works by pushing out your imagination towards something which does not yet exist. Which means, one way or another, however haltingly, you have to form a picture of how you want the future to be.

And once you have imagined, you need to do something else...

Move Your Body Towards What You Want

You cannot blow out a candle with the power of your mind, with visualisation, with invocations or affirmations. It won't happen by thinking it through so that you understand it. Eventually you have to lean forward and blow. You have to move your body towards what you want.

You cannot discover whether you can have what you want by thinking about it or writing in your Journal. The only sure fire way to discover what's possible for you is to move your body towards what you want, relentlessly. Keep at those 1% improvements and you'll soon discover what is possible and what isn't.

Key Points

- Avoid black and white thinking. You have virtually limitless choices for what you do.

- Use your imagination to create your future. Imagine it, then create it.

- Look for 1% changes and keep making them.

- The only way to discover whether you can have what you want is to pursue it. You can't discover this by imagination or thinking about it. You have to act.

Part 6: 12 (Playful) Rules For Knowing What You Want

How are you doing so far? Are you trying too hard to know what you want?

You might like to think about not becoming too attached to the outcome of finding out what you want. I know this is surprising but bear with me a moment. If you take it too seriously, you may block yourself and find it hard to understand your true desires because of the obligation you feel to work it out.

So, here's a checklist, the 12 (playful) rules for knowing what you want. When you know your own mind it's because you are following these rules. Any time you struggle to make up your mind, you're not following one of these rules.

- Play with starting small – make it a daily habit to have an outcome for all the small things in your life **(Step 1)**.

- Watch with amusement as your moods go by and practice asking *what do I want?* instead of *how do I feel?* **(Step 2)**.

- List your bugs and see how many you can squash **(Step 3)**.

- Dwell on what you don't want and then playfully ask *What do I want instead?* **(Step 4).**

- Chop big wishes into chunks. Keep chopping until they are bite size. One mouthful at a time **(Step 5).**

- Notice what you are naturally good at – the things that amaze you when others can't do them as easily as you. You might have found a talent **(Step 6)**.

- Score everything. Use scales. Make up an ideal wheel of life and pin it to your wall **(Step 7)**.

- Sweep the decks so inspiration can land. Remember she's a flighty creature who does not want to soil the hem of her skirt. Make room for her **(Step 8).**

- Learn to live now. Make the most of this weekend. Set out to play with all the things, people, places and contribution that you want **(Step 9).**

- Play with what your senses tell you. Be sensual. See if you can spend a day or two satisfying each of your senses with the most sensual thing you can find **(Step 10).**

- Understand what drives you so that you can say *what's important to me about…is …* **(Step 11).**

- Play with what makes you joyful or has brought you joy in the past. The surest direction for your future is to follow your joy **(Step 12).**

Be lighthearted, uncritical and open minded with yourself without the pressure to come up with an answer. Practise knowing what you want, but make the practice fun.

Knowing what you want is a skill. The more you practice, the better you get.

Not In The Mood?

Remember that anxiety is a sign that you are not focused on what you want. In fact this applies to all strong emotions; anger is a sign that you are not focused on what you want, despair is a sign that you are not focused on what you want. It's even true of physical feelings; feeling full and sleepy is a sign… being grumpy is a sign…

You get the idea.

Anytime you find yourself wallowing in feelings go right back to the beginning and ask *what do I want instead?* Because when you get busy, the feelings will move right along.

In the next sections we take a look at the most common problems you're likely to encounter on the journey to knowing what you want together with a few tips for keeping it going.

Part 7: How To Overcome Resistance To Knowing What You Want

What is the thing that nobody tells you about their success? What is the truth about success that we don't want to hear?

When you first start thinking about what you want and acting with more purpose, it's exciting and that excitement can carry you a long way towards your goals.

You have started making a lot of changes, done a lot of things and even begun to take actions towards your bigger goals. But at some point, like every hero in every story, you may well run into a wall. This section explains why that happens and what to do about it.

When You Run Into A Wall

Does this sound familiar?

Just lately it's become harder and harder to get myself to move forward. It's not that I don't know what I want anymore, I do know, it's just that I find it much harder to actually do anything and its puzzling me.

It almost feels like there is some part of you that does not want you to succeed even though you want to. What you're experiencing is Resistance, with a capital R. Let me try another guess; sometimes, when you get near taking action, it feels like there is a force field repelling you, like the way a magnet pushes another magnet out of the way?

If you have felt any of this, first, you have to understand that this is totally normal and then you have to understand what to do about it. If you haven't yet run into resistance then I have some news for you. It's coming and it's good to be prepared for it when it happens.

Let's see if I can give you a bit of background on what has happened.

How Your Biology Stops You Having What You Want

When you first started to think seriously about what you really wanted in life, you had loads of enthusiasm. Being clear about small things felt really good. As you began to think about more ambitious goals, that felt even better and to your surprise you took some immediate actions, probably more than you originally thought was possible in such a short time.

So you have done the easy stuff, you've enjoyed the process of seeing a new vision for yourself and are now venturing out of what's comfortable towards making bigger changes and taking more meaningful action. What happens when you hit resistance is mostly a result of biology.

Resistance = Biology

Your brain has a simple safety system built with a single purpose – to keep you alive and away from danger. Although it's a simple system, it is powerful because it can override all the other systems when it intercepts a threat to your safety. Imagine a system wide panic button that can do things like flood your muscles with adrenaline, divert blood from nonessential functions (like thinking) and cause your heart to speed up so that you take in more oxygen. This safety system is permanently on duty and anything perceived as a threat will trigger this freeze or flee response.

So even though you might want to start a business, lose weight, volunteer your time, speak in public or work hard on something new, your biology interprets these as threats and marshals every possible stop signal to keep you safe. They are threatening because they are differ- ent from what is known and comfortable. Anything that takes you to the unknown and a possible risk will trigger a signal from this safety system to hide or run away.

At the core of these stop signals is fear. Fear of the new, of danger, of standing out, of possible unseen threats, even fear of ridicule or judgement by others. The more mean- ingful the action, the bigger the likely change it means for you, the higher the fear and the stronger the stop signal.

You Want It But Your Body Is Scared

So, fairly quickly, on any journey towards something new you find yourself in a place where although your mind wants these new things, your body is trying to stop you.

And often, this feels horrible. It's so horrible that you may think you have got the wrong goals. Maybe you've misinterpreted what you really want? It shouldn't be this hard, should it?

I'm afraid that's a myth. In reality, the opposite is true. It might even be like a compass – the more something you want repels you the more meaningful it is going to be for you in the long run. In many ways your unconscious safety system is way ahead of you, it can already see change coming, long before the extent of the change has really dawned on you.

There's another widespread myth. That achieving something new is easy and joyful. Nobody wants to hear about hard slog and they especially don't want to hear that your biggest opponent might be your own fear. When you do hit resistance though, there are several things you can do…

Break The New Thing Into Small Steps That Are Non-Threatening

Whilst it may be scary to pick up the phone to new clients, getting together a list of people to call is not scary. Often if you can start a small part of a new task, one thing leads to another.

Remember your internal threat system is simple, almost childlike. You can reassure it by taking small unthreatening steps that build confidence.

Understand That It Takes Time To Build New Habits

Any new habit – deciding to polish your shoes every week or cleaning out the car regularly or learning to drive or taking up jogging – is hard at first, and then gets easier. Sometimes all your safety system needs is to be shown that it is OK after all. Then, as you get comfortable with the new thing, you become more accepting of it.

Anticipate Resistance

Bigger changes are always going to meet a blizzard of resistance from inside you. Especially those that involve doing something different or possibly exposing yourself to the scrutiny and judgement of others: starting a business, public speaking or putting your creative work on sale. It's inevitable and you should plan for it.

What's also true is that it's only a signal, a warning flag and no matter how strong the repelling force is, once you push on through it you will find that it backs down.

This particularly affects people who constantly do new creative work. If you are going to set out to do something new and different every day then you'll just have to get used to pushing past that initial warning signal.

Follow Your Resistance

One experiment you might like to try is to start each day by working out what you are avoiding or resisting and doing that thing first. It might be an awkward conversation or a piece of routine work or picking up the phone to a new customer or thinking about a new project. Whatever it is, experiment with doing it first.

In this way, you learn to use resistance as a guide to what to do next. Remember, your unconscious safety system is ahead of you. It has often foreseen a change that will stretch you or put you in a situation where you have to perform at a higher level. By deliberately choosing those things you might be choosing to do the things that are going to help you grow the most.

In a perverse and ironic way, resistance might be a signal that what you are thinking about is exactly what you should do. After all if you decided to veg in front of the TV eating junk food and drinking beer you are unlikely to feel any resistance at all. Decide to start Yoga lessons though and you will feel the resistance multiply.

Grind It Out

This is the most damaging success myth of all. Remember all those heroic stories where someone invents a new product or makes a change and their life is wonderful ever after?

Nobody talks about the money running out. The dead ends, the frustrations, the prototypes that did not work, the relationships that got lost on the way. No one talks about the grind. The hours of practice, the constant preparation and training. Somehow, these details get left out of all the stories.

If you know you want something, sometimes the only way is to grit your teeth and grind it out.

Learn To Spot Resistance Coming From Others

Do you remember when we spoke earlier about the reaction from other people once you started showing signs of being more directed and focused in deciding what you want and getting it?

Well I'm afraid to tell you that was only the beginning. Once you get clear about what you want and start going after the really big things, not only will you have to cope with your own resistance, in all probability the amount of flak you get from others will increase as well.

Like crabs in a barrel some of those around you will try and stop you escaping your current life. The worst thing a crab can do is make a break for freedom and sometimes even the people you love will try to sabotage your attempts to change. People going on a diet get offered cakes, smokers struggling to give up will be handed cigarettes, guitarists who start to practice more frequently will be accused of selfishness. Remember that we place far too much emphasis on comfort, safety and security and when those around you see you changing they may reach out to stop it because they, in turn, are scared of what it might mean.

Again, the solution is to push on and show them that the consequences are not as scary as they thought.

Yes, It's A Fight, But You Can Win

You can carry on getting the easy stuff because your body does not see that as threatening. But to get those bigger things you want you will probably have a fight on your hands. To win this fight you might have to push past danger signals from your own nervous system or the well meaning attempts of others to keep you where you are.

If you'd like to learn more about this, buy *The War of Art* by Steven Pressfield (Warner Books, 2003). A fantastic book on defeating your own resistance.

In the end it's down to you. Eventually you will have to choose between mood and desire, between the way your body makes you feel and what you really want. If you want it but your moods and feelings resist madly then you have to choose. Back down or push through. You can treat your resisting feelings as a warning and back away. Or as a symptom of an oversensitive safety system and push past them. In the end it is up to you.

Just imagine for a moment if your life were a bus and you were the driver...

Part 8: Always Know What You Want

How do you keep this up?

Unless you are one of the lucky minority who were born knowing what you want, you will have to come back to this material again (and again).

There will be days when your inner compass spins round and the way seems foggy.

I've found two habits that help to reduce the number of days like this. The first is the habit of **capturing a thought when I have it** and the second is **regular use of a journal** using a technique called 'Morning Pages'.

Let's have a look at how you can make these habits a regular part of your life as you continue to know your own mind.

Capture It The First Time You Think It

One great habit that will help you to know what you want is the habit of capturing any thought that comes into your head so that you can do something useful with it.

Somebody once told me that your brain is for *having* ideas, not *holding* ideas; and that the best way to keep a clear head is shorten the distance between *having* a new thought and *capturing* it.

You cannot control what floats into your head. All sorts of things do and each time a wild idea floats in, your mind assigns it a place in your head and begins to track it. Then, when you are taking a shower or driving or otherwise distracted, these thoughts will ambush you. Why? Because you're now tracking it with a micro part of your attention.

The only way to stop this is to create a management system for all that incoming stuff. And it starts with capture – either writing it down or preserving it in some other form. Then you review it. Then, if necessary, you let it go.

I use index cards for this or pages torn from a small note-book. One idea or thought per card. And I always have a stack of blank cards nearby.

How Cat Food Helps You Know What You Want

Here's an example of how this works.

I've got about 10 cards in my pocket and on one of my cards I have printed **CAT FOOD** right across the middle. Here's why…

On my way to the office this morning I remembered that I need to get some cat food. So I whipped out a card and wrote the thought down, *cat food*. That way I only think about it once.

Of course, writing it down is not the same as actually buying the food but when I get home and empty my pockets, there is a card reminding me about cat food. So I'll add it to the shopping list in the kitchen. When I next go shopping I take my list with me and *tada!* Cat food.

This simple principle of capturing things straight away, so that you only have to thing about them once, is a easy way to clear your head. Let's look at what actually happened:

- I remember *cat food*

- I write it down

- This means I never have that thought again all day

- When I get home I process the cards to do whatever the next step is

Because *cat food* is now on my shopping list I never have to think about it. I only remember when I'm standing in the store looking at my list.

I've achieved two things. I've remembered to get the *cat food* **and** I've kept my head free from the job of holding the reminder about *cat food*.

When You Forget To Capture Your First Thought

Now let's look at what would have happened if I hadn't captured that first thought:

- I remember *cat food* and make a mental note to buy some, but don't write it down

- During my next client meeting *cat food* pops into my head – my brain is reminding me.

- While I'm waiting on the phone for someone to pick up, *cat food* floats up unbidden into my head – another reminder.

- On the way home I'm so distracted by my day that I forget all about *cat food*.

- I'm just about to go to sleep when I remember we have no *cat food* for the morning!

See what's happening here? All that mental energy and space used up to remember cat food when I could have just jotted it down. Remember the bug list and clearing the decks? **Your brain is best used for having ideas, not holding ideas.**

Ten Things That Have Your Attention Right Now

Find yourself 10 blank index cards or 10 small bits of paper. Write down the 10 things that have your attention at the moment – one per card.

Notice what happens. Although writing it down is not the same as doing it, you are slowly teaching yourself that the idea is safe now – this means your brain does not need to keep worrying at it and bringing it to your attention.

You can use anything, a dictaphone, a notepad, cigarette papers. All that matters is that you are always able to capture a thought the first time you have it. It will take a while before your brain totally trusts you to capture things but after a while ideas will drop off your awareness once you capture them.

Capture every thought you have. Just capture them all. Wild ideas, strange notions, product insights, comments, quotes from customers, and then stuff that catches your eye or new ideas you come across. Find a capture system for it all. Build easy capture into your life. Put a notebook and pen in the car, the toilet, tuck some blank cards in your wallet. Do this so that you can take advantage of every fleeting thought.

And then, regularly, make a decision about everything you capture:

- It's something you need and want to do – put it on an action list.

- It's a daft idea you will never do – shred it.

- It's something you might do, one day – start a *might do, one day* list or a *wild ideas* list.

Do this daily if you can manage it but certainly once a week.

Build this habit into your life and nothing will ever get past you. And your mind will stay clear so that you can continue to bring your full attention to whatever you are doing right now. You will become that rare person who is fully present.

You have taught your brain that the idea is safe (so it lets go) and also rewarded it for bringing you a new idea. Your brain likes this. Imagine your brain as a super intelligent person able to make astonishing leaps of insight but with the social skills of a six year old. It likes it when you take note of the ideas and suggestions it brings you. The more you do it, the more new ideas and suggestions will float up from your unconscious.

If you ignore it constantly or make promises you never keep then it will go off in a sulk. Pay attention, note the suggestions down, stick to your promises and you will unleash a flood of insight, ideas, suggestions and connections.

All you have to do to unleash this flood is make sure that wherever you go, you have a way of capturing an idea.

Clear Out Your First Thoughts

This is an exercise made popular by Julia Cameron in her book *The Artist's Way* and it's both simple and useful at the same time. All you do is start your day by writing down whatever is in your head until you have filled three pages.

Eh?

Yes. This morning I got up at 6am, went downstairs, made a coffee, then sat down with a pad and pen and started writing.

I wrote non-stop for three pages and when I'd finished, I walked across to the shredder and destroyed them.

And the point of that was?

Learning To Listen To Your Own Voice

How does a day normally go? From the second you wake up you are assaulted by words, images, contact with other people, information, demands, feelings etc. In fact, for most people there are only two times in their day when they are alone with themselves; just as they are coming awake and just before they go to sleep.

For most, that's the only time when it's peaceful enough to bring to mind anything that has been pushed aside by the busyness of the day. Constantly ignoring this voice will have you up at 3am, finally listening.

Morning pages are a way of deliberately answering the question *What has my attention?* It has lots of benefits but let me go over the basics to point out a few things and see if I can explain why it might be useful.

Do Them Early

First, do your pages early. When you wake up your mind is clear and you've not yet been filled with other people's words and thoughts. Think about it. The second you turn on the TV, radio or read a newspaper or start yelling at the kids to get up for school you are filled with words, opinions, ideas and demands from others. It's easy to forget or miss those things that were on your mind. So do it early. Grab paper and pen and simply write down whatever is in your head.

Total Safety

Second, because you know you will shred them, you also know that no one is ever going to read what you write. This means you have total freedom to write, unedited and uninhibited.

Simply write down the flow of your thoughts. In the morning I'm often grumpy, I need caffeine and I'm moaning. If you saw my pages they are virtually illegible because I write fast, not bothering about punctuation or even correct spelling. You are not writing literature, you are writing anything, about any subject, about anyone, in any way. It's totally liberating and it clears all that stuff out of your head. It's like taking the cork out of the bottle so that you can get at the good stuff.

Do Them Regularly

Third, do this regularly. Remember our discussion about mood and desire. Often I do not feel like doing my morning pages but now I do them anyway. What you're doing with your pages is creating a single, unique piece of work every morning. Once you realise that you can create a new thing, under any circumstances and in any mood, you realise that your creative abilities are somehow separate from how you feel. It is a life changing realisation that your innate ability to create a unique piece of work has nothing to do with the mood you happen to be in. Learning that you can be creative under any conditions is something to carry forward into the rest of your day.

Do Them By Hand

And lastly, do it by hand. Write fast, not worrying about spelling or punctuation. Follow the stream of your thoughts as they come out. Writing by hand on paper is an act of deliberate physical creation, it's just like painting a series of small pictures. Crafting something physical with your hands activates different parts of your mind – especially if you use different colours. The other thing I do is keep some index cards nearby in case I get a reminder or an idea or a To Do I want to keep. Morning pages sometimes stimulate ideas and actions that I don't want to shred – I jot these down on a card so that I can keep them.

Try It

Give it a week and you will see what I mean. Start with a small notebook and fill up three small pages. Work your way up to three normal sized pages. All I can tell you is that routinely writing down your first thoughts in a safe and regular way causes you to pay attention to what has your attention. You will find that what you really want begins to come through loud and clear.

Here are the instructions again:

Pay Attention To What Has Your Attention

Create some time, before the day starts, to write down your first thoughts and keep going until you have filled three pages. Then destroy them. If it helps, start by answering the question *What has my attention?* so that you use your pages to pay attention to what has your attention.

Find Your Origin

Knowing your own mind is the key to being original. You have to know your origin. Morning pages help you know your own mind and as a side effect you will become an original thinker – a person with a view, a perspective, someone who knows what they think. This kind of clarity is both rare and attractive.

Key Points

- To know what you want you need to know your own mind and this won't come from TV or copying friends. It will come when you find your origin, and you'll find this when you pay attention to what has your attention.

- It's by paying attention to those thoughts hovering at the edge of your awareness that you will stay focused on understanding what you really want and finding the motivation to go after it.

Part 9: Using Your Holiday To Set Goals That Work

How *do* you set goals that work (once you know what you want)?

Have you ever failed to go on holiday, planned it, booked it and then just procrastinated or sabotaged yourself? No, of course you haven't. I'm willing to bet that, barring external events, you've hit your goal every time.

Why? How can you plan, organise and deliver a holiday to yourself but not hit lesser goals in your life? How is this possible?

What's Different About Your Holiday?

You manage to get your holiday because you're off duty (it's not an official goal) and in this relaxed state you fall naturally into using the instinctive goal getting process that you were born with. It goes something like this:

- You get the holiday urge and kick this thought around with yourself and with others

- You begin to imagine what it will be like. You keep doing this, with yourself and maybe with others. A clear (ish) picture emerges and you know what you want and begin looking forward to having it.

- A random series of ideas, suggestions, to do's and things to prepare all come shooting into your head. Even when you are not expecting them. You find your thoughts return to your holiday in idle moments.

- Eventually you start sorting all this stuff out, putting it in a rough order, thinking about what needs doing first, what steps depend on each other – *Must renew passport first because that takes six weeks. Travel agent wants final payment a month before we go* etc.

- You start doing things about it – no longer thinking but acting. You check your progress.

- You hit the deadline – there you are at the airport with luggage and passport at the right time.

- You do all of this without hesitation and without the help of a seminar, self-help book or coach.

Make Every Goal Like Your Holiday

To get more of your goals, make sure you are using this natural and intuitive process you were born with.

- Know what you want and why you want it – this might take some time.

- Imagine the final result and make sure that it's something you actually look forward to having.

- Stand by for the rush of unstructured ideas, hints, to do's, reminders etc as your mind leaps around the problem, connecting it all up and identifying loose ends. A good response to this is to capture everything without judgment.

- Sort your thoughts out, put them in order, work out what needs doing first and what things depend on each other.

- Act. Do something. Make the first call. Write the first note. Have the first meeting etc.

- As you act, keep going back to your imagination of the final result and making sure that you are on track. Adjust as necessary.

- Hit your deadline – right place, with the right stuff ready to enjoy the result.

Relax. You are good at this stuff. If you can get yourself on holiday then you already possess the skills to get anything you want. Imagine it. Collect ideas. Sort the ideas out. Act. And it's yours.

Part 10: Frequently Asked Questions About Knowing What You Want

Nearly all of the questions from people who struggle to know what they want boil down to two big ones:

- *What do I do when I just don't know?*

- *Is it OK to know what I want – isn't it just selfish?*

Let's cover these now:

What To Do When You Just Don't Know

If you've put the exercises in this book to work then days when you just don't know will be a distant memory. Occasionally though you'll find yourself completely stumped and if that happens here's how to deal with it:

- Breathe. Go outside and take loads of slow lungfuls of fresh air. This will release the tension of not knowing and send lots of fresh oxygen to your brain.

- Pay attention to what has your attention. Forget all about knowing what you want and pay attention to whatever is ringing your doorbell at the moment. When you've dealt with that you will find your mind clears enough to know what you want.

- Let yourself off the hook. Remember that not knowing what you want is a bad habit but one which you were once skilled in. Sometimes you slip back into that old skill and that's OK for a while. Just don't stay there.

- Ask yourself *Whose agenda am I working on?* and make whatever changes you need. All the time you ignore your agenda you will be working on someone else's agenda. Do you really want this?

- Whatever is happening, ask yourself *What Do I Want, Instead?*

- Give up your search for The Answer. There isn't one. It's a series of answers, big and small. Isolate the small things you want and do those. Practise the skill of knowing what you want and the bigger questions will resolve themselves.

- And finally, remember that it's not about how you feel but about what you want. And these exercises can help you with that, over and over again.

But Is It OK To Know What I Want?

It's a fair question. When does knowing what you want start to become a cover for selfishness or being totally me-centred?

And it can, make no mistake. History is littered with charismatic people who were crystal clear about what they wanted and did great damage to everyone in the process. How do we avoid this on a smaller scale in our lives?

The fact that you are asking the question is a good sign. Let's see if we can clear it up.

Start with that history I mentioned. When we see clarity in others we often call that charisma and we venerate it because it seems so different from our personal experience of the world. People who know what they want appear to have answers that we don't and so they often attract followers.

Sadly, history also shows that thousands of people were willing to follow charismatic individuals intent on causing harm. Why? Partly because most people are slightly passive and compliant, living with no clear agenda of their own. If you act like a sheep it's easy to abdicate decision making to some shepherd who appears to have answers. It lets you off the hook for having to take any responsibility for your life and choices.

This is a strong argument for more people knowing their own mind and acting accordingly. If these habits were more widespread then charismatics intent on harm would find it less easy to find willing followers. Knowing what you want and being willing to act on it prevents you being swept away by others who may have a harmful agenda for you.

Looking after yourself properly is the best way to look after others. To love your neighbour as yourself is to give them a raw deal unless you have taken care of yourself first. It's hard to hold the rest of the human race in high regard unless you also give yourself high regard. One way of doing this is to pay attention to your own needs and how you can meet them. Then you'll be able to help the rest of the planet with theirs.

Reread the section on Mood and Desire. Our moods may lead us to want things that are unethical or harmful or selfish especially if we navigate by asking ourselves how we feel. (I want chocolate, immediate gratification of every whim and to avoid anything scary.) When we focus on our deepest desires though, our wanting tends to be ethical, helpful and beneficial to all. We get there by understanding what we want (not how we feel).

Remember too, there is a difference between knowing what you want and acting on this knowledge. You will want to think carefully before you act on what you want because, sensibly, some of it will involve disruptive changes to the way you live now. What you want is not going to go away, though. It will bug you until you give it some attention, so you might as well gain this kind of clarity now.

The most generous thing you can do for the world is to find your own niche and do your thing to the best of your ability. That's what we need from you.

And, of course, you are unique. Never again will there be anyone quite like you. You have a unique place here on the earth which you occupy only once. You have only one life and one way to make it count is to begin to listen closely, see clearly and feel deeply for who you are and what you should be doing.

So, go figure it out and then go after it. It's huge fun.

First, Know What You Want

Here's a reminder of all the tools and tips we've covered.

Part 1 – Remember what it's costing you not to know your own mind

Part 2 – Decide that you will know what you want. Make this your first decision.

Part 3 – Understand why it is so hard to know what you want

Part 4 – Twelve Steps To Knowing What You Want

Any time you are stuck because you do not know what you want, you can:

- Start Small – spend a day making deliberate, conscious, but small, decisions about what you want to reconnect with your internal compass.

- Follow Your Desire, Not Your Mood – it's not how you feel, it's what you want

- Make A Bug List – scribble down a list of what's bugging you right now. Pick one and deal with it.

- Use What You Don't Want – rehearse what you don't want and ask yourself *'what do I want instead?'*

- Make A Dream Come True – take the time to break a dream into tiny actions. And then do one.

- Uncover A Talent – notice what is easy for you. Grow these skills and abilities.

- Keep Score – check your wheel of life. What would make for a smoother turn?

- Clear The Decks For Inspiration To Land – deal with mental clutter by removing physical clutter.

- Live Now – bring forward something you have been putting off.

- Stop Thinking And Come To Your Senses – notice what your senses are telling you.

- Work Out What You Value Most – and put yourself where you can satisfy this value

- Follow Your Joy – pick something that brings you joy and go do it.

Part 5 – Get 1% Closer To What You Want. Take baby steps.

Part 6 – Twelve Rules For Knowing What You Want.

Part 7 – When The Going Gets Tough – beating your own resistance.

Part 8 – Always Know What You Want.

Part 9 – Use your holiday to set goals that work.

Part 10 – Frequently asked questions about knowing what you want.

Imagine this. You wake refreshed after a good night's sleep because you hit your bed just when you wanted to. As you think about the day ahead, a clear list of what you want begins to organise itself in your head. You spend a moment or two sorting through it and then you are up and off, eager to get hold of the day and make it yours.

At work or among friends, people know they can trust you because when you say 'yes' it means 'yes' and when you say 'no' it means 'no'. You've noticed that, somehow, you are working less but achieving more. This may be because you only pick the things you love to do and you do them with all your heart.

To your surprise you notice people following your lead and it reminds you of something. You remember a time, not so long ago when you had no agenda; so you followed people who seemed to be clear about what they wanted. Several people have asked you to help with their goals and you always start like this.

"First, you have to know what you want. Let me show you how…"

Afterword: What Really Works?

I'd hate for you to think that my life is one long celebration of clarity and insight. It really isn't. I'm firmly in the 95% who struggle to know what they really want. I was raised negatively, to look at the downside and I'm an Away From person. It's always much easier for me to move away from something than decide what to move towards. I tend to let things get bad before I do something about them. And when I do choose a direction, I regularly experience the fear and resistance that comes from setting out to pursue what I want.

So I'd thought I'd close by telling you what really works for me, on those days when my inner compass decides to spin aimlessly. Your mileage may vary. Here are the things that always work for me:

- Learning to tell the difference between mood and desire, between how I'm feeling and what I want.

- Being smart enough to intervene when my feelings are running out of control and panicky voices invade my head. There really is a difference between how I feel and what I want. Picking desire over mood is a ninja move.

- Abandoning a traditional To Do list and writing each item on a separate card or piece of paper really works for me. It means I can sort them easily and focus on them one at a time. I practise ubiquitous capture because it works.

- I always know what I want in the next 10 minutes and sometimes that is enough. After a while, you can fill a whole day like this.

Someone told me that you can't become a runner by reading running magazines (unfortunately). You have to run if you want to be a runner. Write if you want to be a writer, sculpt if you want to be a sculptor. When I'm stuck, it's funny how often that is also a literal description of what I'm doing with my body – sat still, holding my breath, staring at a screen. Sometimes starting to move (any movement) is what helps to sort out congested thoughts.

And when nothing else works, I pick something small and do the very next thing in front of me.

When you find out what works for you, please let me know. You can mail me on andrew@lighthouse365.com. I read everything sent to that address.

Recommended Reading

Pressfield, Steven *The War Of Art* Warner Books, 2003. Hands down the best book ever on resistance and self sabotage. You'll come back to it time and time again.

Cameron, Julia *The Artist's Way* Pan Books, 1995. A 12-week course in recovering your own creativity by helping you to know your own mind.

Brande, Dorothea *Becoming A Writer* Jeremy Tarcher, 1981. Even if you don't want to be a writer this is a short and fascinating introduction to training your brain to help you know what you want

Allen, David *Getting Things Done* Piatkus, 2001. I highly recommend GTD as a way of managing all the lists and thoughts you have generated. Will help you to set up a number of practical habits for achieving what you want.

Allen, David *Ready For Anything* Viking, 2003. A series of short, digestible essays on making things happen.

Walsh, Peter *It's All Too Much* Simon & Schuster Ltd, 2008. A guide to keeping the clutter you want and letting go of the stuff you no longer need.

Neill, Michael *You Can Have What You Want* Hay House, 2006. Once you know what you want, this is the place to go. Michael is a genius at helping you put your goals into action.

Sher, Barbara *I Could Do Anything, If Only I Knew What It Was* Delacorte Press, 1994. A practical guide for those who find a single goal too constricting.

Landsberg, Max *The Tao Of Coaching* Harper Collins Business, 1997. Learn the art of conversational coaching from this great little book

Godin, Seth *The Dip* Piatkus, 2007. When you hit a hard patch, how to sort out whether it's a blind alley or just something temporary.

Buzan, Tony *MindMaps For Kids,* Thorsons, 2003. A great, easy, direct introduction to using mind maps as a way of capturing and organising your thoughts. Try mindmapping your answers to the exercises.

Grab Your Free Bonus

Head to *www.firstknowwhatyouwant.com* and give us your email address. We'll send you the **'First Know Journal'** that accompanies this book and keep you in touch with updates. It's free to join and you can unsubscribe at anytime.

Printed in Great Britain
by Amazon.co.uk, Ltd.,
Marston Gate.